MAKING THE BREAK

MAKING THE BREAK

First steps in overcoming

- ▼ Eating disorders
- ▼ Pornography
- ▼ Drugs
- ▼ Alcohol

David Partington

Harold Shaw Publishers
Wheaton, Illinois

© David Partington, 1991, original edition under the title *Kicking It.* Harold Shaw Publishers edition, © David Partington, 1992, is published by special arrangement with Inter-Varsity Press, 38 DeMontfort Street, Leicester LE1 7GP England.

ISBN 0-87788-522-2

Cover design by Paul Turnbaugh & Associates

Library of Congress Cataloging-in-Publication Data

Partington, David, 1944-
   Making the break : first steps in overcoming eating disorders, pornography, drugs, alcohol / David Partington.
     p.   cm.
   Includes bibliographical references.
   ISBN 0-87788-522-2
   1. Habit breaking—Religious aspects—Christianity.
2. Compulsive behavior—Religious aspects—Christianity.
3. Christian life—1960-
I. Title.
BV4598.7.P37   1992
248.8'6—dc20   91-38054
                                             CIP

---

99 98 97 96 95 94 93 92

10 9 8 7 6 5 4 3 2 1

*To my dear wife, Sue,
and three fine sons,
David, Andrew, and Matthew.*

Contents

Introduction

Passion and conviction have been essential to the writing of this book. Passion in my desire to see broken and wasted lives totally liberated, and conviction that this freedom is not only what God wants, but that he has sacrificially provided the resources for it to become a reality—in every hopeless situation.

I didn't realize it at the time, but the first draft of this book was more of a textbook and, consequently, would have been of use to only a very few people. It has developed, I believe, into a short guidebook that I pray will help many. Its brevity will, perhaps, provide a surge of real hope to those who have dependency problems. Its simplicity may encourage those who are helpers to see that the problems are not as mystical or technical as they may have come to believe.

This book is written, above all else, out of the experience of seeing broken lives totally transformed by the redeeming love of God, active through his Spirit, his Word, and his people. Faith demands that I trust in God's mysterious nature, but his love, revealed in completely redeemed lives, creates only hope, joy, and expectation of what else he plans to do.

Thanks are due to so many people who have not only encouraged me, but who have provided the physical environment for me to work in—Tom and Margaret Moyle, Spencer and Grace Naish, and Eddie and Linda Boss. Aid was graciously given by people from Yeldall Manor, who not only read my manuscript but gave understanding, support, and love. Sheila Poynter at Yeldall Manor worked hardest of all as she patiently and uncomplainingly typed the manuscript from my appalling scrawl.

You, the reader, must be the judge of whether this book achieves its real purpose. I only pray that, at the very least, it will result in you coming face to face with God's love, tenderness, and purpose for your life.

David Partington

1

*A*lways on your mind

When twenty-three-year-old Carter Cooper hurled himself from his mother's Manhattan penthouse balcony crying, "What's it all about?" he was speaking for many young adults today. Britain's *Sunday Times* newspaper said, "His question still hovers uncomfortably in the air, crying out for an answer" (July 31, 1988).

Suicide seemed like a pretty wild response. Carter, the son of Gloria Vanderbilt, had everything to live for: a first-rate education, his own exclusive New York apartment, and an excellent job. Despite all this, since breaking up with his girlfriend some months before, he had been receiving psychiatric care. He had nothing to live for.

Carter was a little different from many people who don't get as far as actual suicide. He just couldn't face himself. Reality for him was an aching emptiness inside, feelings of inadequacy, failure, and deep-rooted rejection. Feelings that, like many of us, he'd been struggling to avoid for most of his life.

As Eileen Orford, a counselor with London's Tavis-tock Clinic, puts it, "If a child has been brought up with very materialistic values, without having his own feelings valued, he is particularly vulnerable to an emotional kick in the teeth."

▼ Under pressure

Many people can identify with Carter's final, heart-rending cry, but few will actually commit suicide.

And the fact is that so much of the despair and futility is found among the young people in society. While some will call a help-line, many more will carry on, bottling up the frustration and pressure. They learn to live, uneasily, with their emptiness and dis-satisfaction. Somehow they tolerate the sense of failure, knowing that they will never attain the true potential of their lives. "I've grown used to feeling this way," confesses one young woman. "I can hardly im-agine life any other way."

Others, far more restless, will be driven to compen-sate for their inadequacy by a desperate quest for symbols of happiness. Realizing they can't change their feelings, they change their circumstances: a more dynamic job, a more attractive partner, a larger house or car. "Tired as I was," admitted one young executive, "I felt pressured to do anything to block out my true feelings."

Some even use people to compensate for their over-whelming feelings of rejection. Casual liaisons are entered into, and partners are cast off like old boots when they can't deliver the goods. Other people will demand only long-term, intense relationships, where they only *give* love when they *feel* loving. Long-term or short-term, the deep-seated rejection is reinforced, because nobody has the capacity to give at the level demanded. Eventually they settle for mediocrity and shallowness from others and give equally in return.

Compassion and selfless love (which bring true joy and contentment) are sacrificed, available only in the ad-man's fantasies.

At the end of all compulsive, almost manic, grasping there is, for a large number of people today, only the sad, stark reality of Carter's words: "What's it all about?"

The answer for many is simple: "Nothing—there is no point. We are all insignificant—we are all going to die." As the book of Ecclesiastes in the Old Testament of the Bible puts it, "It is useless, useless . . . Life is useless, all useless. . . . Everything leads to weariness—a weariness too great for words. Our eyes can never see enough to be satisfied; our ears can never hear enough" (Ecclesiastes 1:2, 8, *Good News Bible).*

▼ Hooked on pleasure?

Another group of people deal with the question "What's it all about?" in a different way from those who choose suicide, settle for mediocre relationships, or mask their feelings with possessions. These people cope with the same emptiness, inadequacy, failure, and rejection by blocking out these feelings or by refusing to face reality. They cope with the questions, pressures, and decisions of life by avoiding them. They, like others, have felt deeply let down by the shallowness and emptiness of today's beliefs, values, relationships, and lifestyles. But, unlike others, they have discovered certain desires, pleasures, and habitual practices that mean they don't have to face up to their problems or find answers.

I call these practices *compulsive* or *life-dominating dependencies*. They are an everyday part of life for more people than we would ever imagine. These people are, to use Archibald Hart's term, "Addicted to Pleasure." He goes on to say, in his article of the same name,

> Every day millions of people engage in activities just because they give them pleasure. They seem to be "hooked" on work, sex, food, money, gambling, fighting, religion, relationships, and even certain types of thinking, because they feel stimulated and experience positive mood changes whenever they engage in these activities. And, when they are deprived of them, they experience great discomfort. *Christianity Today*, December, 1988

Food disorders
Seeking after pleasure through normal activities sounds innocent enough, surely. Yet an innocent activity can turn into a nightmare. "Anna," for example, went on a 200-calories-a-day diet while at her university simply to lose weight. Yet, as an article in *21st Century Christian* reports, "After a few months of such rigid control, Anna found the urge to eat insatiable, and started binging." Even worse was to come: "Unable to make herself sick she swallowed handfuls of laxatives to get rid of the massive amounts of food she could consume during a binge."[1]

Pornography
Anna's compulsive dependency problem is described as *bulimia nervosa*, but there is no "technical" term for the problems described by Bill Hybels in his book

Christians in a Sex-Crazed Culture. He quotes from a letter he received:

> I'm thirty-four years old, and I can tell you truthfully, I was in bondage to desire for twenty-five of my thirty-four years. Most specifically in the area of pornography. It was an addiction as powerful and as seductive as any deadly drug, only slower and more subtle in its effect.

The writer of the letter goes on to describe how it all started when he was six years old, how he went on to meet "the most beautiful girl I had ever known. She had the physical attributes that I had grown to adore. She was a year and a half older than me. It was love at first sight for both of us, and the combination of her beauty and her unselfish love kept me from diving head-first into the sexual underworld." Eventually, however, the slide continued, to the point where even "X-rated movies" and "several hundred magazine mistresses" did not satisfy him and he was trapped by the need for even more thrills.[2]

Drugs

Seeing the term "hooked on pleasure," many would still relate compulsive dependency to drug addiction or alcoholism. We're used to reading stories about people like Stan, who acquired a taste for drugs as a curious teenager. "Curiosity turned into addiction," a local newspaper reported, to the point where "he broke into chemists and drove hundreds of miles to sign on with dozens of doctors." Then Stan started drinking heavily, "washing down handfuls of pills with crates of liquor each day. At his peak he was taking one hundred pills a day."

Mike's story, in the same newspaper, reinforces the picture we have of drug addiction. Having been educated in a convent, Mike, whose parents split up at an early age, first started popping pills as a teenager. "Eventually a friend enticed him into trying heroin. Through naive innocence he did. Soon he was hooked, trapped in a nightmare lifestyle that degenerated into overdoses, crime, prostitution, and prison."

Tranquilizers
Such stories seem a long way from quiet, leafy suburbs, yet an increasing number of people have become the victims of "professionally created dependency." In 1989 a British newspaper reported that "More than 500,000 people may be addicted to the tranquilizer drugs." The same article, based on a report published by the Association of Community Health Councils, went on to say, "More than 3 million people are estimated to be 'chronic' users. Yet benzodiazepines do not 'cure' anxiety or insomnia." Taken gladly from the doctor "to enable them to cope during a crisis," these pills have trapped as many as one in twenty people in a compulsive dependency equally as horrific as heroin addiction (*The Times*, July, 1989).

Alcohol
For one student, who prefers to remain anonymous, alcohol dependency started much as it does for an increasing number of young people today—at a party.

For the rest of the year I got smashed every weekend. The highs felt so great, especially in contrast to the lows I felt during the week, that I sought them again and again . . . till drinking and partying had become my two most important pursuits in life." *HIS*, December, 1986

▼ Imprisoned by habit

No one is safe from finding themselves with a compulsive dependency problem. It can strike anyone, regardless of class, personality, race, creed, intelligence, or financial background. And certainly no one struggling with dependence is alone.

The workaholic in the country is driven by the same desperate need to succeed as someone in a large city. The anorexic housewife from middle-class suburbia is trapped by the same desperate habits as someone in an urban setting. The alcoholic who drinks three bottles of sherry a day is striving to blank out the same pain as the homeless "wino" on the streets of Sydney, Hong Kong, New York, or London. The gambler who plays the roulette wheel in Las Vegas exhibits the same lack of peace that marks the person who bets on the greyhounds in Glasgow.

Not one of these people sets out deliberately to become compulsively dependent. But, whether they flaunt their problem or seek agonizingly to keep it secret, they are trapped by something that is outside their immediate control.

Much as they would long to be different, to be free, to be normal, they are in a deep pit with slippery sides, no rope and, seemingly, no one to help them out. Much as they long to break the compulsive and often degrading habitual behavior they have become dependent upon, they don't believe it will ever be any different.

Yet still they long for some respite from the pressure. To get up tomorrow and know he won't drink a bottle of spirits before 10 A.M. To know that she won't gorge enough food for two days only to vomit it away before her husband comes home. To know they won't use the housekeeping money to gamble instead of buying their youngest child a pair of shoes. To know she won't sell her body again just to get her fix. To know he won't break his promise yet again to be home for junior's birthday this year because he needs to work late.

The prison of dependence

Trapped by the need to put their own needs first they don't really think it will ever be different. Like James Ditzler, they can say that despite having spent little or no time in prison their addiction is "stronger than any wall or iron bar. I took my prison with me wherever I went, even though I deluded myself I was free. I was caged tighter than any lion or prisoner in solitary confinement."[3]

Most people in this situation wanted to break out of their prison a long, long time ago. And it wasn't that they didn't realize what was happening. They felt self-hatred for what they were doing to themselves and other people. But it still felt good, it still brought relief, it blocked out the inferiority, or the deep-rooted rejection, or the frustrated dissatisfaction. Relief from gnawing emptiness was far more important than facing up to the truth of what they had become and all the pain they had caused to those they loved.

Of course, there were times when they came close to giving up, not least when they ran out of money or someone they loved threatened to walk out. In situations like these the reality overcomes the desire, and a determined effort can result in a real freedom. But stopping doesn't remove the physical or mental pain they feel. Facing up to their responsibilities only confirms their sense of inadequacy, their inability to relate fully to people or the agony of their emptiness. So, even if the paycheck isn't due they know that someone, somewhere would still lend them money. The threat of a loved one leaving fades into insignificance against the craving to meet their need in the only way that brings relief.

As people surrender themselves to drugs, drink, pornography, or whatever else, the realization hits them that they are willing to sacrifice anything to meet their needs: family relationships, including children; long-term career prospects; friendships that go back a long way; self-respect; honesty; hard work. Anything that they have built their lives on can just be thrown away.

They have hit rock-bottom. But even the implications of this fact can be masked or blanked out by more drugs, more drink, more work, bigger bets, harder porn, more gorging, more vomiting, more abuse, more of anything.

▼ Are you hooked on pleasure?

"If you think you have a dependency problem, you probably have." This phrase is often repeated by the experts. If what you have read so far seems familiar in any way, then the reality is that you are likely to have a compulsive dependency problem. If you have, then I'm thankful that this book, while talking realistically about the problems, is also written in confidence that there is a real answer. I've seen enough lives changed from years of addiction to heroin and alcohol to be excited about you making the break. I've heard about, and seen, enough people who have been liberated from life-dominating dependency to food disorders, pornography, and relationships, to know that nothing can "separate us from the love of Christ" (Romans 8:35).

The secrets of success

The first step for every person released from dependency was total honesty alongside a realistic attitude toward themselves and their circumstances. Being truthful to themselves about their dependency problem, more than anything else, was the turning point. Like everyone who joins Alcoholics Anonymous, these people built on the experience of hundreds of thousands who have become free through admitting "We are powerless—our lives have become unmanageable." Being able to talk openly with someone else was also part of breaking free, whether it was sharing with a friend or seeking help from a doctor or support through an organization like Alcoholics Anonymous.

The second life-changing step for many was to recognize the simple and powerful truth that God loves us deeply and has a perfect and special plan for our lives. "'For I know the plans I have for you,' declares the LORD, 'plans to prosper you and not to harm you, plans to give you hope and a future'" (Jeremiah 29:11).

God, more than anyone else, wants us free. Unlike others, however, he doesn't just give advice or support, he gives himself—totally and completely in Jesus. *God isn't interested in simply setting us free from our dependency, he wants to set us free from everything that made us dependent.* His commitment to us is total—he wants to give us a completely new, dynamic life lived in his strength, power, and presence.

Do you have a life-dominating problem?

The following questionnaire is designed to help you determine if your life has tendencies toward compulsive, habitual behavior. Realism is the beginning of the road to freedom for many addicted people, so answer each question honestly.

Circle the number that applies to your answer.

☐ *I have felt increasingly depressed for some time now.*
True
False

☐ *I have become more irritable over recent months.*
True
False

☐ *I no longer mix with the same people that I did a year ago.*
True
False

☐ *I spend an increasing amount of time thinking about one particular thing in my life.*
True
False

☐ *I am unable to share about myself with anyone.*
True
False

☐ *I tend to demand perfection from myself.*
True
False

☐ *I tend to demand perfection from other people.*
True
False

☐ *I am attracted to articles and books about a particular habit I am involved in.*
True
False

☐ *I have felt that my life is being increasingly controlled by one particular need or habit.*
True
False

☐ *There are some habits I am involved in regularly that would be of concern to people I love.*
True
False

☐ *I find myself taking more risks about being discovered.*
True
False

☐ *I find myself lying increasingly about my behavior to people closest to me.*
True
False

☐ I know my behavior in one particular area is wrong but believe I am justified.
True
False

☐ *I find I dislike myself more and more.*
True
False

☐ *I find that my own pleasureable feelings are increasingly more important to me than other people's feelings.*
True
False

☐ *I find that certain areas of my life are uncontrollable.*
True
False

▼ How did you score?

Score 2 points for every "True" answer. Add up the points and check your total score against the summary below:

20–32—you are showing some compulsive behavior tendencies and should talk with someone you trust about what you think may be a problem.

12–20—it is unlikely that you have any problems, but if one particular problem gets increasingly regular, then talk with someone you trust.

0–12—it is highly unlikely you have a compulsive dependency problem.

2

The slide into dependency

L aura was only thirteen when she smoked cannabis at a party "just for the fun of it, because the other folks were doing it" (*Family Circle*, December, 1989).

Daisy looked at a friend and saw how thin she had become. Describing her response in *Woman Magazine*, she said, "You look at yourself, see how much fatter you are. You try to lose a few pounds to catch up and it turns into something nasty."[1]

▼ Starting on the slide

The innocent way in which Laura and Daisy started confirms how most people begin to slide into compulsive, or life-dominating, dependency. Laura went on to become a drug addict while Daisy's story describes the terrible journey into anorexia nervosa, which is all too frequent today.

Other people have begun the slide into alcoholism because their friends persuaded them to have "just one more drink."

Life-dominating dependency on hard pornography began for some men because they were bored and lonely.

Redundancy, grief, depression, and other problems lead some to visit the doctor and, within months, find themselves on the "tranquilizer scrap heap."

Gambling addiction has broken more than one family simply because someone risked the family's savings on a "sure winner."

Once we've started, for whatever reason, we carry on because we've experienced instant gratification— we feel good. We have been hearing the message proclaimed for years: "If it feels good, do it." If you have a headache—take an aspirin. Can't sleep? Take a sleeping pill. Under pressure? Tense? Have a long, slow drink. Bored with the same, dull routine? Take a holiday. Prevented from achieving promotion? Back-stab someone. Need sex? Use whoever is willing.

We can experience instant gratification at any time. We feel good, so why not enjoy ourselves—just one more time?

▼ Out of control

Irregular use slowly but surely becomes regular use. Low-key experiments increase to become habitual behavior. Attitudes become reinforced, often by other people involved in the same compulsive dependency. Anyway, why say no when we are now able to communicate with the opposite sex without feeling embarrassed? Why stop increasingly rigid dieting when we sense envy or admiration from others? Why say no when the pills enable us to enjoy added excitement? Why say no when gambling involves more dynamic company? Why say no to even more work, when additional responsibility brings additional money and status beyond anything we thought possible for ourselves?

▼ Tormented pleasure

By now we're in a twilight world, between normal life, as it used to be, and an ever increasing compulsion to do those things that, on the one hand are exciting and yet, on the other, are leading us into something we can't control. We recognize the risks to ourselves, but, like Laura at the beginning of the chapter, fear and excitement get mixed up.

> There was an element of danger to the stealing, for Laura, which became a "high" in itself . . . there was the companionship of friends . . . going to parties and discos. The days passed in almost dreamlike succession, with the need to get the drugs the one focal point of life. It couldn't go on, but although there were moments when she was tormented by the thought of how deeply she was sinking into addiction and crime, Laura couldn't stop. *Family Circle*, December, 1989

The point at which we can't or won't stop is the point where we have slipped over from habitual use into compulsive or life-dominating dependency. On the one hand we feel compelled by something outside of ourselves, while on the other we find it irresistible to deny ourselves the pleasurable feelings we have become accustomed to. If our problem is drink, for instance, we have become alcoholics. We started off as social drinkers and progressed to being problem drinkers who needed to drink more and more to experience the same effect. The drink affected every aspect of our lives. Now, in the final stage, we no longer control drink, but the drink "controls" us. Our tolerance has developed to the point where we must keep drinking in order to avoid the mental, physical, and emotional discomfort of withdrawal.

An anonymous drinker put it this way: "I basically denied or ignored the damage my drinking habits caused to my body, to my sense of self worth, to my relationships, and to my reputation." In "The Secret Life of a Student Alcoholic" he writes,

> During the next three years, I walked through swamps in formal wear, awoke in strange places, got myself thrown out of classy bars, abused friendships, and collected an array of hangover experiences. *HIS*, July, 1986

▼ Trapped by self

Our needs and habits dominate not only our own lives, but the lives of other people. But the consequences (either to us, or them) we disregard almost totally. James Ditzler sums it up well in *Living in the Day*:

> Selfishness epitomizes the addict of whatever kind. I, self and me, becomes a way of life and so it was for me. I always had to do what I wanted and woe betide anyone who interfered with my plans.[2]

No one would even try to forecast that they would reach such depths as Anna or Steve did. Whether we describe them as compulsively dependent or addicted is almost an irrelevance; their condition was a tragedy.

Anna had reached the stage where she was so depressed that she would cut her arms with a razor. "Then my whole mind is centered on my arms and the pain, and not on what I've just eaten."[3]

Steve wrote that he had come to the point as a drug addict where "I used to keep out of my children's way as much as possible because it hurt me to see them and not be able to help bring them up as I should."[4]

▼ Are you on the slide?

Why have so many people become addicted? What happened in their lives to make them get into the habitual behavior that is distorting and corrupting their lives?

Young people

Adolescence is the most critical time of all for being prone to sliding into dependency. It's that time when the "highs" seem highest but the "lows" can't go any lower. It's the time when we are desperately seeking to establish an identity and yet everything around us seems to conspire to put us down. All too often we see the love of parents as conditional upon the results of exams or a certain kind of behavior. Instead of being accepted for ourselves, we're compared unfavorably with other young people. Life seems to involve countless arguments about the wrong type of clothes, beliefs, music, and friends.

It's all summed up in the life of someone we'll call Roger.

Mom and Dad didn't mean to make growing up more difficult than it was. It's just that they were too busy coping or surviving. By the time they got home they were too tired to show me the attention I know now that I needed. When I failed an exam, they got uptight for my sake, because they wanted me to be able to make choices. They meant well, but I was left with the feeling that I needed to be someone different to be loved by them.[5]

Growing up, for many, also brings with it the realization that some parental relationships are less than loving. All too many homes are actually split, and teenagers, in particular, often feel guilty that it happened.

Outside of the home, teenagers look at a world that is materially better off than at any time in history, and yet is totally lacking in moral absolutes and standards.

Even close friends show acceptance one day while ignoring them the next. Most will agonize, almost daily, as they painfully compare the often inflated sexual experiences of their friends with their own unfulfilled experiences and relationships.

Little wonder, then, in the midst of so much confusion, that boredom, curiosity, and peer pressure are the prime reasons that so many teenagers and young adults start into drugs, drink, porn, and other dependency problems.

Older people

We might expect that increasing maturity would reduce the pressure for many people's compulsive dependency. But the reality is that age brings its own particular set of circumstances that leave people dangerously open to sliding into problem behavior.

Children fail to live up to the high investment of parental time, money, and caring. More than this, they develop some of the same "flaws" of character that typify their parents' lives. This reinforces the fact that the relationship with a husband or wife really has failed to live up to the expectations and demands that the other has made. Accidents and illness can bring major pressure, while the death of loved ones in later years also brings the need for anything at all that will enable people to cope with the grief.

Housewives often feel desperately trapped by the necessity to satisfy the needs of a demanding young family. Others feel cheated by husbands who come home too tired to provide the selfless love and support they need. Some mothers, as well as single women caring for dependent parents, may be frustrated and angered by circumstances that prevent them from becoming the unique individuals they feel they have the right to become. Relationships in which both partners work can grow cold as they are only able to see each other at the end of the day.

The material prosperity and security many have worked so hard to achieve, often at the expense of close relationships, has failed to bring the measure of fulfillment that has been "promised" by the advertisers. Instead of getting easier, the working environment becomes more stressful. All too often older men and women find themselves "passed over" for promotion or written off and given retirement as soon as they turn sixty-five.

▼ Anything to fill the vacuum

Bill Hybels writes:

> We live in a world of cheap, quick thrills. You can get a quarter pounder in less than two minutes, guaranteed. Sit on the couch and with a punch on the remote control, turn on the music, the T.V., or the VCR. Take a pill and, within minutes, clear out your sinuses, settle your stomach, or lose your appetite. It's all so simple. Partake and dispose. A thrill or a cure a minute.[6]

This confirms that whatever vacuum exists in our lives, young or old, there is something waiting to fill it—good or bad. I'd like to look both at *why* so many people are open to filling their empty lives with garbage *and* at the good news about release.

▼ On the outside looking in

I've been able to stand on the outside "looking in" at life-dominating dependency and compulsive behavior for over ten years now. Most of that time has been spent developing and directing the drug and alcohol rehabilitation program at a place called Yeldall Manor. It would take another book to communicate the desperation of all the lives I've been involved with. It would take two books, at least, to tell you what's happened in the lives of those that God has set free and transformed.

I've also been on the inside of life-dominating dependency, having had a problem myself. It's been this experience, which I'm not proud of, that has also given me a sense of realism about the problem and God's methods and answers to bring about total deliverance and freedom.

Some of the people quoted in this book have spoken frankly of the chaos and despair of their lives. They haven't tried to ignore their failure or responsibility before people or God. In fact, it's because they have found real freedom that they have been able to be absolutely honest about themselves while also being open about finding answers where they least expected.

▼ Discovering a way out

Steve, who wrote, "I used to keep out of my children's way as much as possible . . ." could talk later on about his remarkable release:

> About five in the morning I couldn't sleep. I had a strange feeling come from my head and through my body. Someone was telling me, through my own voice, that I wouldn't need drugs or alcohol again. The withdrawals stopped, and tears were running down my face—they were tears of joy. I felt stronger than the pain that had been in me and I knew I had a chance of new life.[7]

It may sound easy, but anyone involved will tell you that letting go of compulsive desires and habits is always more difficult than carrying on, no matter how desperate you are. But it can and does happen—people not only find complete freedom, but a purpose and conviction beyond their own needs.

One man whose life and family had been all but crushed and broken beyond resurrection had to fight hard to allow the new life in him to have control—he still does. But a report from the professional instructors at Outward Bound speaks volumes as to the reality of change that can come about in the life of a "junkie."

> He was willing to put others before himself and his support was appreciated by all. His selflessness was evident in his dealing with another group in the Center. They were mentally handicapped and thus had a difficult time at meals. M—— always stayed to help them. He did this in his own time and commented several times on the pleasure it brought him to help others.
>
> M—— achieved a wholly exceptional level of success personally and as a group member. The course proved difficult, but his determination never wavered. He was awarded the Principal's badge from Outward Bound, a rarely given token of his outstanding performance.

Tough love achieves miracles that I've seen in the lives of people dependent upon drugs and in the lives of others, too.

Another man became deeply embroiled in pornography, partly, he said, because "I always was a dreamer, who often fantasized as a teenager." He even went on to become a church leader while still deeply involved in the grip of pornography. He later found

freedom in the reality of God's love through working
with those who had drug problems!

▼ What about *you*?

It doesn't matter where you are on the slide, there is
always hope. It starts with being realistic with yourself and facing up to the truth instead of the lies that
you have been telling yourself for so long.

Make up your mind now to read the rest of this
book, not because I say so, but because you are
making up your mind to start looking for answers.

Better still, keep reminding yourself of the verse in
the Bible that says, "Everyone who calls on the name
of the Lord will be saved" (Romans 10:13). Why not
call out now, right where you are, and ask a loving
God for help to set you free?

▼ ▼ ▼

Co-dependency—buzz word or real problem?

Co-dependency is a word that is being used increasingly by many different people to describe those who have a compulsive dependency *and* the people around them—family, friends, or "professionals."

There is no strict definition of what co-dependency means, but it appears to cover three definable groups:

1. Members of a family who live, for instance, with an addict or alcoholic.

Christianity Today explains it as follows:

> In the families of alcoholics, the system revolves around the alcoholic as family members protect and enable him or her to continue the alcohol abuse. Each family member becomes involved in a collusion of sorts that requires massive emotional energy. December, 1988

2. Those who work with, or care for, someone with a dependency problem.

They can themselves be over-dependent on the need to help people who are addicted. Their own self-worth and sense of identity is directly related to working with those in need.

Again, *Christianity Today* states:

> They are often passive-aggressive, lacking in trust, angry, rigid, controlled, and self-centered. Poor communicators, they may have problems develop-

ing intimacy in relationships and handling their sexuality, and they often repress feelings and thoughts. Many are perfectionists who feel power-less, hopeless, withdrawn, and isolated.

3. Co-dependency can also relate to the growing self-help movement such as Alcoholics Anonymous, Over-Eaters Anonymous, and many others.

Members can sometimes value and need the group so much that they don't want to "get better." That would mean leaving their security.

▼ Are you co-dependent?

With these definitions in mind, helpers and those close to someone with a problem should check their own motives and needs. We may be making things worse despite all our efforts. How do you feel when a sufferer begins to see relief? Do you need to be needed? Where would you focus your life if the person close to you were to recover fully?

3

Who's to blame?

Drugs can dull and degrade a person,
but thank God, they can never erase
the indelible traces of God's image in his life.
Within minutes of meeting these people
one catches a glimpse of what
they were intended to be.
It is this glimpse, recognized and cherished,
which provides a basis
for truly respecting them.[1]

We live today in a desire-oriented society. There has never been an age where people's desires have been so corrupted and distorted by so many messages from so many different directions. In fact, a whole industry, advertising and marketing, has developed over the last twenty years, dedicated to using every conceivable means to raise our expectations to fever pitch, so we will respond beyond our "normal" inclination.

Virginia Larsen in her article, "Games Eaters Play," writes,

This industry has created the myth that every itch deserves to be scratched, every twinge anaesthetized, every appetite gratified, reinforced by so much advertizing. We have a horror of unsatisfied desires the way that nature abhors a vacuum. We discriminate very little among cravings, sensations, appetites, and hunger. Our inclination and our conditioning is to silence them all by giving in to them. Have a headache? Take . . . Can't sleep? Try . . . Hungry at 11 P.M.? Order a pizza. Thirsty? Run down and get a Coke.[2]

▼ Spoiled brats and fake answers

Is it so surprising to us then that an estimated four out of ten people are addicted to something? Why are we so surprised when we read, "Your son is fifteen. He lost his virginity two years ago, swills Carlsberg Special Brew, and slouches in front of the television . . . His sister is much the same. Both cherish ambitions to earn pots of money; neither cares a lot about the environment, poverty, or the family" (*Sunday Times*, January 14, 1990)?

The article, based on a report entitled *Spoilt Brats* by Gold Greenlees Trott, a leading advertising agency, goes on to paint a depressing picture of a whole generation and concludes, "By the year 2020, a generation of children will be more screwed up than any generation before them."

Small wonder, then, that people become compulsively dependent, because no one can even begin to meet the desires and expectations that have been created in people's minds. So while pills, whether taken secretly or because they're prescribed, don't

solve any of the real problems, they do blank out the
emptiness. Alcohol, of itself, changes nothing, but
taken in excess it can filter out the unwelcome
problems of living. Dieting or overeating, to excess,
do cause dramatic health problems, but can also
bring a sense of comfort and control over one's
circumstances. Pornography, at any level, degrades,
but it can also bring a form of escape from the disap-
pointment of mediocre or missing relationships.
Gambling often brings deprivation and distress, but
it can add excitement to a dull, boring existence.
Drugs have a long-term, disastrous impact on every
aspect of life, but they do cushion people from having
to accept responsibility for the apparent failure of
their own lives.

▼ Distorted family life

My mother died when I was in second grade. The
only thing that made me feel warm and loved after
that was a stomach full of food. Consequently, I
overate consistently for the next three and a half
years until my father remarried. Food was a mother
substitute for me.[3]

Thankfully, not too many people go through the experience, described by Virginia Larsen, of losing their
mother so young. However, many of those with life-
dominating dependency problems do seem to grow up
in a family environment that leaves them wide open to
unhealthy influences in their lives. A survey completed
by the Lions Club International Drug Awareness Program among 3,500 young drug users and their families
came up with the following facts:

- They all had problems communicating with their families.

- They all had experimented with drugs that had been offered to them.

- Three-quarters could not communicate well with their fathers.

The survey also confirmed that many drug users were pressured by parental demands to do well at school—to be successful.

▼ Afraid to love

It's all completely opposite to what God intended. John Powell, in his book *Why Am I Afraid to Love?* sums up what all children need:

Only when the bud of the flower receives warmth from the sun and nourishment from the mothering soil will it open and expose all of the beauty latent within it. So, too, the human person at the beginning of life must receive the warmth of human love, assurance, and the nourishment of parental affection if it is to open and expose the unique beauty that God has placed within every human individual.[4]

Experience confirms that where there is the failure to receive that love, then most people will meet their needs on a physical level. They will do anything they can to shut out the reality of not being fully cherished and accepted. Lawrence Crabb puts his finger on the issue:

When the desired goals are not reached we are motivated to protect ourselves from the painful feelings of insignificance and insecurity. Alcoholism, compulsive spending, over-eating, excuse-making, many psychosomatic ailments, some forms of schizophrenia, and a host of other behaviors are often designed to anaesthetize or compensate for the emotional pains of feeling worthless.[5]

This is another way of saying we will do anything to block out the painful feelings. And once we have found something that will do it, we give in to our evil desires and set off down the slide into dependency, absolutely certain that we can get off anytime we like.

Tragically, it's only when life has gone completely out of control that many people begin to look for the answers in the right place.

▼ Finding real answers

It is clear, therefore, that society, expectation, a lack of love, parents, and many other factors have contributed to the web of dependency that traps so many people today. This should be no surprise to us. Ever since Adam and Eve the effects of sin have been felt by everyone. "For *all* have sinned and fall short of the glory of God" (Romans 3:23, italics mine). Or read in Romans 1 about how healthy desires have become distorted and twisted. It is for this reason that the Bible concentrates so much on the importance of good family life and secure relationships (Ephesians 5:1-4). Someone with a compulsive problem is the last person who needs reminding that others have let him down.

But this is not the whole picture. When you take out the failings of others and their effect upon us, we, too, are responsible for our sinful actions—our "falling short of God's glory," his best. As we stand at the scene of the crime of our compulsive dependency, our habits, practices, actions, and choices all mean that we are implicated also. Even if it is other people who have failed us by handing us the loaded pistol of our past, it is we who have fired the fatal shot.

David's story

Take, for example, the mighty King David and see how desire can become corrupted and lead to things that were never dreamed possible.

David's slide all started innocently enough one evening when he "got up from his bed and walked around on the roof of the palace. From the roof he saw a woman bathing. . . ." (2 Samuel 11:2). The Bible goes on to make it clear that the woman was beautiful and so David sent someone to find out who she was.

It's important to note that up to this point there is little, if anything, that seemed to be a major problem in David's life. He had been brought up as the youngest son in a God-fearing home. He had served the previous king, Saul, with great willingness, and his faithful friendship with Prince Jonathan is legendary. He had written some of the greatest poetry of all time, poetry that revealed a deep sense of the knowledge of God. He was a brave warrior and leader, and by the time he saw Bathsheba bathing, a great king. But, whatever he may have been, David still sent someone to bring Bathsheba to his palace, and we can reasonably question his motives even at this stage. The Bible is short on detail about what followed, but we do know that David, knowing that Bathsheba was married to Uriah, "slept with her."

Not many people today would question David's behavior—it happens all the time. But that doesn't make David's actions, or ours, right. What we are looking at is how evil desire led David to do something that wasn't normal, wasn't acceptable, and was so totally out of character. In fact, virtually everything that David was and believed in was sacrified, simply because he chose to give in to evil desire. Common sense, logic, and restraint were thrown overboard in a lust and an obsession that totally overruled everything else in his life. And he still didn't feel satisfied.

But it didn't stop there. David was so consumed by desire that news of Bathsheba's pregnancy resulted not only in his plotting to kill her husband, Uriah, but actually involving others in his sin.

No one is safe
If someone like King David could allow evil desire to take control, so that adultery and murder are valid options, then no one is safe from evil desire.

Maybe we've tried to convince ourselves that sin isn't our problem. Other people have told us that we're not really that bad and all we have to do to put things right is work on our good points. We try hard, but in the end we get tired because it's impossible always to be good on our own. So we give in to our desires, give in to pleasure at any cost, determine to enjoy ourselves more and more. Yet we never experience the satisfaction and fulfillment we are looking for.

Given that we have chosen to turn our backs on God and go on sinning, that society has raised expectations in us it can't meet and, in some cases, our families haven't had the resources of love to give us—who is going to love us enough to break the chains that are wrapped so tightly around us? The answer is God. It can only be God because he alone has the resources to meet both our physical needs and provide the real love that will bring the security, significance, and fulfillment that each one of us needs.

▼ The Father heart of God

Has it ever crossed your mind that God really does want to be involved intimately in your life? Have you perhaps shut God out from your thoughts simply because you believe you are not important enough, or not worthy enough? God cares for you, desperately, in a way that Floyd McClung summed up so well when he wrote,

God is constantly thinking an uninterrupted stream of loving thoughts towards you as though nobody else in the world exists. You say, "How does he do that? How can he be personally involved with billions of individuals at the same time?" I don't know, but I know it's no problem for the Creator of the world. Who knows how he does it? Just enjoy it!

Your parents were often preoccupied with their activities, and sometimes showed no vital interest in the small events of your life, but God is not that way. He cares. He is a God of detail. Why does the Bible say that God has numbered the hairs of your head? Not because God is concerned with abstract mathematics. He's not a computer wanting data. This picture is trying to tell us in what sort of detail he knows us and cares about our lives. . . . Do you have any idea how attractive you are to God?

One of the biggest hindrances to him is when we feel our flesh is repulsive to him. When my small son is covered with mud from the back yard, I pick him up and clean him off . . . I reject the mud, not the boy.

Yes, you have sinned. Yes, you have broken God's heart. But you are still the center of God's affections—the apple of his eye. It is *he* who pursues *us* with a forgiving heart.[6]

▼ Christianity as dynamite

Lawrence Crabb continues the story of God's never-failing love for us:

The apostle Paul was not ashamed of Christianity because it was dynamite. It transformed dead people into live people, weak people into powerful people, and empty people longing for significance into deeply fulfilled people satisfied with the real purpose and importance available through Christ. Paul hints at the Christian resource for meeting significant needs in Romans. In the first chapter and twenty-first verse, he tells us the first wrong turn that people make which leads to utter degeneracy and personal death: they fail to glorify God as God.

God is glorified when I humbly bow before Him, acknowledging His right to run my life, and bring myself into line with my Creator as his obedient creature. Accepting Christ's death as payment for my sins puts me in a position where I can center my life in the context of his will. I am alive to him, indwelt by the Holy Spirit, who works in me "both to will and to do of *his* good pleasure" (Philippians 2:13, *King James Version*). Now each moment of life, each unit of behavior (getting out of bed, playing ball with my kids, kissing my wife) can be seen as part of a larger meaningful whole. The context of my life becomes the external purpose of the sovereign God of this universe.[7]

▼ Gloriously attractive to God

Whatever background we have come from, whatever society we have grown up in, whatever family we have been brought up in, God loves us enough to leave the choice to us of whether we go his way, in his strength and power, or carry on trying to meet our needs our own way.

However, taking God's way involves facing up to personal responsibility for the wrong choices we've made and leaving God to deal with all the wrong things, however bad, that others have done. Whether we do so or not, one thing is sure—everyone will, one day, stand before him to acknowledge his Lordship and be judged. "For," as the Bible says, "he has set a day when he will judge the world with justice by the man he has appointed. He has given proof of this to all men by raising him from the dead" (Acts 17:31).

We do have freedom of choice, and change is possible. I've seen it happen, time and again, to those whose lives were written off because they were addicts, alcoholics, because they were constantly consumed by lust, had anorexia, gambled.

But life-dominating dependency wasn't the end for them but the beginning, because they were low enough to call out to God.

"As the Scripture says, 'Everyone who calls on the name of the Lord will be saved' " (Romans 10:13).

Choosing God means that life takes on a whole new dimension as we learn to walk with God the Father, God the Son, and God the Holy Spirit. It's not an easy walk, but it is dynamic, exciting, and totally fulfilling if we will choose God and serve others.

▼ ▼ ▼

Acceptance

Oh, to know acceptance
  In a feeling sort of way,
To be known for what I am
  Not what I do or say.
It's nice to be loved and wanted
  For the person I seem to be,
But my heart cries out to be loved
  For the person who is really me!

To be able to drop all the fronts
  And share with another my fears,
Would bring such a relief to my soul,
  Though accompanied by many tears.
When I find this can be done
  Without the pain of rejection,
Then will my joy be complete
  And feelings toward self know correction.

The path to feeling acceptance of God
  Is paved with acceptance on Earth;
Being valued by others I love
  Enhances my own feeling of worth.
Oh, the release and freedom he gives
  As I behold his wonderful face—
As Jesus makes real my acceptance in him,
  And I learn the true meaning of grace.

A pity it is that so late we find
  His love need not be earned;
As we yield to him all manner of strife

A precious truth has been learned.
Then, as we share with others who search
  For love, acceptance, and rest;
They'll find in us the Saviour's love
  And experience the end of the quest.

Charles Solomon[8]

4

Making the right choices

There will be no major solution to the suffering of mankind until we reach some understanding of who we are, what the purpose of creation was, what happens after death. Until these questions are resolved we are caught.
WOODY ALLEN

You have made us for yourself, and our hearts are restless till they find their rest in you.
AUGUSTINE

Blaming other people for the condition we're in can make us feel better. It also gives us a false sense of security. But it changes nothing. Bitterness toward God, our parents, probation officer, teacher, husband, wife, girlfriend, or boyfriend can justify a lot of wrongdoing, but it still means we're trapped in dependency. Blaming circumstances, the fact that we didn't go to the right school, didn't go to college, didn't get the right job, can ease the pain for a while, but it doesn't make any significant difference, except to keep us trapped in our present situation. Nothing, in fact, makes any difference until we make the right choices and accept responsibility for what we are.

▼ Hope in the pigsty

Sitting in a pigsty doesn't rate very high as a good place to come face to face with reality. It's not the most comfortable, hygienic place, whether you like pigs or not. But for one person at least, it was the beginning of life as God intended.

The prodigal son, described in the Bible (Luke 15), would probably have gone through the whole process of blaming other people, circumstances, and maybe even himself, in order to justify sitting in a pigsty. He knew he was quite justified, by law, in having taken a half share of his father's land. He may have believed that his father had only been protecting his own interests in trying to persuade him to wait before selling the land. He had certainly convinced himself that it had been important to leave home and the dull, boring farming community where he lived. Important, perhaps, in order to stretch his mind and learn something of the wider world.

It appears from the story that this son had let the fast-moving, exciting life in a new country take control, but he might have reasoned that even this was because he had been "overprotected" by his parents. But perhaps the biggest reason why he was sitting in a pigsty was his so-called friends. It was they who most likely had encouraged him to spend all his money and then, when it had run out, they ignored him totally. The final straw was the famine, which had come along when he was completely broke. Couple that with living in a strange country with no lasting friends, and was it any wonder he had to take the job of feeding pigs? It must have been difficult for him, a Jew, to conceive of doing a worse job than feeding pigs.

Yet sitting in a pigsty forced him to face the reality of his true condition. He decided to start off by going back home. To accept his responsibility and to say he was sorry. It wasn't that he expected all his rights, because he knew he had no right to be accepted back as a son. Even so he would see his dad and ask if he could be a hired servant. That way he wouldn't have to carry on sitting in a pigsty, waiting to starve to death. He would also be close to his father, his family, and everyone else he knew.

Life's toughest choice

None of it could have been easy. Even leaving the pigsty would have been difficult because at least there he got some food, and there was some security. He must have been doubting the wisdom of what he was doing almost all the way back. Would he make it home in one piece from this far and distant land? Would he be accepted? Perhaps feeding pigs was better than being laughed at because he had failed. The closer he got to home the more he must have known he deserved nothing but rebuke, anger, and rejection, and yet—"while he was still a long way off, his father saw him and was filled with compassion for him; he

ran to his son, threw his arms around him and kissed
him" (Luke 15:20).

What a staggering turn-around. What an incredible
result—his father had been waiting eagerly all the
time! How much his father must have loved and
missed him to be watching—to see him so far off. Yet
there was still more, because, far from being given the
job of servant he asked for, he was accepted back,
fully, into his place as a son. His father even or-
ganized a party so that everyone could see how
delighted he was to have his son back.

Starting back home

For each and every prodigal, like you or me, who has
grown tired and weary of the consequences of his or
her own choices, there is always the option of touch-
ing base or returning "home" to the Father. But first,
like the man in Luke's story, we have to respond to
the quiet stirring within us and make the choice to
face up to circumstances as they really are, before
starting back home to God.

It never is easy, but whatever doubts you may have
about leaving the security of your current existence
behind you, they will soon be lost in knowing that
God, your loving Father, has been looking out for you,
ever since you chose your own way. He has actually
been waiting all the time for you to return. He hasn't
been waiting to rebuke or condemn you, but to restore you to full inheritance—as his son or daughter.
Whatever the poverty and degradation of your life, no
matter how many times you've binged, vomited, used
heroin, committed adultery, gambled, filled your mind
with pornography, there is always the freedom to
return to God as your Father.

▼ Ransomed, healed, restored, forgiven

For some people, it happens in prison, for others in a dirty alley or even in an airplane. They not only reach the conclusion about the utter futility of their condition but make the decision to begin to put things right. It happens to different people in different ways, but always, at the point of despair, God moves in response to heartfelt cries.

No one is beyond God's love to restore. However unacceptable you may feel you are, you can always start back home to God. No one is beyond his care, because the loving arms of Jesus are always outstretched to welcome you, to encompass and enfold you. It really is true what the apostle Paul wrote:

> For I am convinced that neither death nor life, neither angels nor demons, neither the present nor the future, nor any powers, neither height nor depth, nor anything else in all creation, will be able to separate us from the love of God that is in Christ Jesus our Lord. *Romans 8:38-39*

But there's more, because when we respond to God, the consequences are always better than we dared to hope for. As an educational psychologist who became anorexic at the "unusually old age of twenty-eight" wrote:

> It was a case of "psychologist heal thyself" and I couldn't and I knew enough about psychotherapy to know that no other psychologist or psychiatrist could either. So I struggled on until, at the age of thirty-two, I reached the point of utter despair. On

the point of suicide, but unable to think how to do
it, I sobbed out "Help me! Help me!" and immediately the room was filled with the presence of God—
I knew that God was there and that he loved me.
The experience was so real to me that never, since
then, have I doubted his continual presence with
me and his love for me.[1]

▼ Free to choose

Many, many other people I know can confirm that
hitting rock bottom was not the end, but the beginning for them. The beginning of a totally fresh, new,
dynamic life. But, in the same way that we aban-
doned our lives to our own selfish desires in the first
place, we need to abandon ourselves to God. It doesn't
mean that we have got to put every single thing right
immediately; it means simply that we have got to
respond to God in the way he clearly indicates—just
as we are. As Isaiah said in the Old Testament: "A
bruised reed he will not break, and a smoldering wick
he will not snuff out" (Isaiah 42:3). God doesn't want
us perfect, just willing.

William Russell, who describes himself as a "Law
School Alcoholic," woke up one Sunday morning,
having spent "the most horrible week of my life,"
during which he had clearly sensed his separation
from God for the first time.

> As I passed the mirror and looked in I was revolted
> by what I saw. I showered, still very shaky, put on
> my clothes and went to church. The message I
> heard in church that day changed my life. It was
> the message of Jesus and his offer of salvation to
> all. The pastor made it clear that each of us has a

choice to make—either we receive God's gift of salvation by grace through Jesus, or we continue in the death that results from our sin. Through that pastor, God made it clear that I wasn't a sinner because of my alcohol problem, but I was an alcoholic because I was a sinner and separated from God. The message was sobering. I responded by receiving Jesus and committing my life to him. *HIS,* April, 1982

▼ Abundant life

Making the choice to return to God and being accepted back is something very special, but it really is only half of what God has planned for us. We can be free of any kind of compulsive dependency because God's freedom is not found in what we are now but in what God created us to be.

It is true that only God can fully meet our needs, but it is also true that he is in the business of *transforming* our lives through his life. He has already chosen to do certain things that mean we need never be the same again. As always, however, he leaves the choice to us as to whether we accept them and move in the freedom they bring.

In his image
First, he created us in his image to reflect his character. "So God created human beings, making them to be like himself" (Genesis 1:27, *Good News Bible*).

Far from being just castoffs of society, we were created by the Creator to be caretakers of the world in which we live. We were created not only to know about God but to be creative and to understand— deeply. We were—are—made for fellowship with God,

and through this, to know the highest level of fulfillment through glorifying him with all of our lives.

Many people would find it difficult to conceive of a
man injecting into his groin because all his other
veins had collapsed. They would find it even more
amazing to see that same man, only a year or two
later, helping delinquent young people find a true
purpose in life. You can't actually tell just from looking at him what he used to be like compared with the
radiantly healthy but serene individual he is now. He
doesn't shout about what God has done in his life,
but when pressed he will tell you quietly that knowing
God on a daily basis is better than any "hit" ever was.

Created for a purpose

Second, we were created specifically by God for his
highest purposes.

> You created every part of me;
>> you put me together in my mother's womb.
>> you saw me before I was born.
> The days allotted to me
>> had all been recorded in your book
>> before any of them ever began.
>>> *Psalm 139:13, 16*, Good News Bible

The truth is that we are not some accident of life
but unique individuals with unique personalities. We
are created by God for a special relationship with
himself and other people—to bring about God's purposes in their lives.

Outside of God's plan, there are many who have
become sad, pathetic shadows of what God created
them to be. Yet lives that have been broken by booze,
drugs, gambling, anorexia, and perversion have been

transformed utterly. Individuals who once would have put all their energy into nursing their habits and meeting their desires have become writers and artists, gone to college and passed degree courses and held down demanding, responsible jobs. They have also become fine husbands, wives, and parents and have contributed as much to the society that once rejected them as any "normal" person.

Abundant life

Third, we were created to have eternal life. "For God so loved the world that he gave his one and only Son, that whoever believes in him shall not perish but have eternal life" (John 3:16).

We were created not to be restricted by the limitations of our own, or other people's, understanding but to know life from God's perspective. There is nothing about the past that can be excused or justified, and few of those who have found freedom from compulsive dependency try to do so anyway. Instead they have found their security in God's eternal plan for their lives. Though they are often aware of the frailty of human nature because of their own mistakes and failures, it is this that gives them a very beautiful sensitivity to other people's needs. They recognize that they are living on borrowed time, but that time doesn't end in death but in life—God's eternal life.

Filled with the nature of God

Fourth, we were created to "bear the likeness of the man from heaven" (1 Corinthians 15:49), by being "filled to the measure of all the fullness of God" (Ephesians 3:19).

We are called to be the reality of Jesus to others. To be his smile to those who are sad. To be his gracious-

ness and gentleness to those who are hurting. To be
his healing hands to those who are sick. To be his
love to those who are lonely and forgotten by a busy,
self-centered humanity. There cannot be a higher
calling or anything more dynamic, exciting, and fulfilling, and it's all ours when we make the choice to
turn to God.

No matter how broken or how deformed we may be
emotionally, mentally, and physically, by addiction of
whatever description, all this, and more, is God's
desire for our lives. God hates the sin of dependency
in the same way he hates any sin. He longs for us to
be free from its power and living in intimate relationship with him.

▼ Free to fail

Fear of failure is often the direct cause of most life-
dominating dependency problems. Success and the
need to "perform" to a certain level has haunted many
of us for most of our lives. We tried so hard to be what
our parents, teachers, bosses, social workers, or
probation officers wanted us to be and failed. Society
is so success oriented that anyone who fails, and
keeps on failing, is ultimately rejected, ignored, and
even shunted somewhere out of the way, where he or
she won't be an embarrassment.

You can't be a bigger failure, in the world's eyes,
than hanging dead, nailed on a cross. Jesus, however,
chose to fail, not out of some moronic stupidity or
some robotic response to circumstance, but because
saving us was more important than succeeding in the
eyes of men and women. Jesus, the Creator of the
universe, had the choice *not* to fail in the world's eyes.
We can see this so very clearly in his heart-rending

cry, "My Father, if it is possible, take this cup of suffering from me!" (Matthew 26:39, *Good News Bible*). At the same time he went on to make the choice that was to bring the opportunity for total freedom for you and me: "Yet not what I want, but what you want."

God sees us at our worst
Jesus chose failure as far as the world is concerned. But through it all, he not only defeated the power of sin *in* our lives, but also broke the influence of other people's sin *upon* our lives. Through the cross he put us into that same relationship that he had with his Father. Today, you and I can look the fear of failure directly in the eye and know that its power is utterly defeated. We can accept failure because God not only accepts and loves us totally, but will not allow anything ever to come near us again that we can't cope with—as long as we keep our eyes firmly fixed on him. We have entered into a completely new state of life described by Lawrence Crabb:

> My need for security demands that I be uncondi-
> tionally loved, accepted, and cared for, now and
> forever. God has seen me at my worst and still loved
> me to the point of giving His life for me. That kind of
> love I can never lose. I am completely acceptable to
> Him regardless of my behavior. I am under no pres-
> sure to earn or to keep his love. My acceptability to
> God depends only on Jesus' acceptability to God
> and on the fact that Jesus' death was counted as
> full payment for my sins. Now that I know this love
> I can relax, secure in the knowledge that the eter-
> nal God of creation has pledged to use his infinite
> power and wisdom to ensure my welfare. That's

security. Nothing can happen to me that my loving God doesn't allow. I will experience nothing he will not enable me to handle. When problems mount and I feel alone, insecure, and afraid, I am to fill my mind with the security-building truth that at this moment a sovereign, loving, personal, infinite God is absolutely in control. In this knowledge I rest secure.[2]

▼ Always on my mind

I learned the reality of these words in my own life when I realized that I had to stop asking God to make me "feel better" because I could never succeed—on my terms. I had spent fourteen years, even as a Christian, expecting God to adjust people and circumstances to suit my feelings, my needs, my desires. All it had brought was frustration, anger, and bitterness, with the result that my Christian life was empty and almost irrelevant.

Having gone totally "down the tube" and become compulsively dependent, I tried very, very hard to justify that I had the right to do what I wanted. I told myself that God had no right to rule my life, and anyway, if he really loved me he wouldn't have let me fail. I had all but succeeded in justifying my behavior to myself, if not to other people.

Yet the harder I tried to lock God out, the more he showed me he loved me. It wasn't only that I could not intellectually dismiss him, but that other people just kept on loving me when all I had done to them was reject them and cheat them. The end came one evening in a hotel. I was on a business trip and had failed to pack a book to help me to get to sleep. Frustration led me to pick up the Gideon Bible from the bedside table. With nothing much to do, I read through the index and turned, out of curiosity, to the passage marked under "backsliding." The words of the psalm I read didn't condemn me, but rather I felt a deep sense of hope.

> Have mercy on me, O God,
>> according to your unfailing love;
> according to your great compassion
>> blot out my transgressions.
> Wash away all my iniquity
>> and cleanse me from my sin.
> For I know my transgressions,
>> and my sin is always before me.
> Against you, you only, have I sinned
>> and done what is evil in your sight,
> so that you are proved right when you speak
>> and justified when you judge. *Psalm 51:1-4*

With the knowledge of God's holiness, and my own sin, came a deep sense of unworthiness, and yet, with it too was a sense of total acceptance and unearned love. What really gave me hope as well were the words, "Restore to me the joy of your salvation and grant me a willing spirit, to sustain me" (verse 12). Not only could I know forgiveness and joy, but God's Spirit would actually help me to choose his way and break free of the need to put myself first.

▼ From failure to freedom

It was a long road back to real freedom, with many regrets for the way I had hurt so many people. But I had the growing knowledge of God's desire to bear the burden with me. Increasingly, I found that I no longer wanted circumstances to be changed or other people to treat me in a certain way. For the first time I could accept that problems and difficulties were not the enemies they had always been. More than this, there grew in me a deep sense of peace in knowing that not only was God going to use difficulty and pressure for my well-being but for the well-being of others, too.

Choosing failure, on God's terms, not only brings healing from the past for us but also for others. The fact of Christ's victory is not only relevant to our wrongdoing, but it cuts the power of other people's sin over us. We can be free of the way in which other people have treated us or failed to treat us. It's not that they are now irrelevant, but we can now separate their actions from them as human beings and therefore love them because God brings his healing for all they have done in failing us.

When we choose God on his terms, he fills us with his Holy Spirit so that we are enabled and equipped to live his life out for other people. We have that same power to use in building God's kingdom in the lives of others that he used "when he raised him [Christ] from the dead" (Ephesians 1:20).

A chance to change

The staggering reality of God's love is that, because we are "filled to the measure of all the fullness of God" (Ephesians 3:19), then other people that the world has written off as failures will find the love and security in us for which they have been looking so desperately.

Honesty about ourselves and our real situations is more than the beginning of the end—it's the beginning of a totally new life—if we accept it on God's terms. Let me ask you to pray the words below so that you, too, can experience God's forgiveness through Christ's death on the cross and the healing God wants to bring about in your own life:

Father God,
I want to start back home to you. Please forgive me for my sins, for living life for so long on my terms. Thank you for creating me the special, unique person that I am and for sending Jesus to die so I can be free of the past. I ask you to fill me with the Spirit of Jesus and I choose to serve you as Lord of my life. Amen.

▼ ▼ ▼

Defeating compulsive dependency in twelve steps

I have revised the steps that Alcoholics Anonymous uses with alcoholics to provide a specifically Christian approach to help defeat any compulsive dependency problem.

Step 1. We choose to admit that we are powerless to defeat sin in our lives, and therefore our lives are unmanageable.

Step 2. We choose to believe in a holy God whose love has defeated sin and whose power can transform our lives.

Step 3. We choose to accept that Christ died for our sins before rising again, and we ask him to rule in our lives.

Step 4. We choose to allow God to show us ourselves as we really are and how he created us to be.

Step 5. We choose to acknowledge where our lives fall short of God's glory.

Step 6. We choose to ask God to transform those defects in our character through the power of his Holy Spirit.

Step 7. We ask God to continue to reveal our sin for what it really is and to allow Christ's resurrection power to defeat it.

Step 8. We choose to ask God to show us clearly all those people we have harmed and to help us willingly to make amends to them.

Step 9. We choose to make amends directly to anyone who has done us wrong, whenever possible, except when to do so would injure them or others.

Step 10. We choose to make amends to others in the power of the Holy Spirit, even when the cost to ourselves is painful.

Step 11. We choose, through prayer and reading God's Word daily, to know more of Christ and the power of the Holy Spirit.

Step 12. As we experience the richness of God's love and acceptance, we choose to set others free by loving and serving them at the cost of our own needs.

5

*P*ractical steps and spiritual breakthroughs

I have been involved with people who have compulsive dependency problems for far too long to say glibly that breaking free and living a life of freedom and fulfillment is easy. Yet I've seen broken men and women, people the world wrote off a long time ago, totally transformed.

Almost without exception, they all came to the end of their ropes. They all came to that place where they cried out to God. But it was here, at the lowest point of their lives, that God not only saved them but richly blessed them (Romans 10:12-13). Noel, and many like him, can confirm that at the height of his drug addiction he was vicious and mean, trampling over anyone who got in his way. Noel cried out to God in prison in utter desperation, but having cried out he thought that, yet again, nothing was going to happen. Then he said, "I felt like I was a tiny kid in my father's arms, secure, safe and loved, all of me—unconditionally."

▼ The beginning of the end

From that point on, even though Noel had accepted Jesus into his life, it wasn't the end of his problems. It was, however, the beginning of an exciting, dynamic life where Noel found out that God would take all his "wasted years and use them for good." Noel went on to marry Marge and spent three years in Bible college. He became a Baptist minister and worked for a time in one of the worst inner city areas. Now he's back at Yeldall Manor in England, leading a team of residents into the same freedom that God gave to him.

John's story

Another person I have grown to love, John, was a failure as far as the world was concerned: an addict, a junkie, not worth worrying about. One newspaper reported what John had learned about himself: "Heroin took away the feelings I found hard to deal with—inadequacy and insecurity." The report went on to say that John's twenties were very vague and that while "everything seemed to be free, it turned around until I was my own prisoner." The story continued:

> John's lifestyle brought an almost inevitable series of personal disasters. His marriage at twenty-four to a fellow addict lasted less than three years. He also lost his daughter. His wife took their daughter to the United States. He believes he will never see them again. *Reading Evening Post*

There were even more disasters after that until John cried out to God one day that he had no friends. "God spoke to me and said, 'If you want a friend for life, here I am.' I broke down and wept for two or three weeks."

Shortly after this John came to Yeldall Manor, where he went through our tough program. Even when he left, a year later, he went through a difficult time while learning to live a totally new lifestyle. But God has worked miracles, not only in John's transformed life, but in bringing the daughter he thought he had lost back from the States, and in providing him with a lovely wife, Kathy. Now God has given John a deep desire to communicate those hard lessons he has learned to others who are trapped in bondage. And all because John cried out to God and gave him his failures, which then became opportunities for Christ's strength to break through.

This book is written out of the privilege of living, learning, and working with Noel, John, and many, many others. The lessons were learned the hard way. We talked for hours about the solid and exciting principles of Christian discipleship in counseling and teaching sessions, but then they had to be lived out in the painful reality of putting them into practice in everyday life. We laughed about the joy and blessing, and we wept over the difficulties and the disasters.

▼ Fulfillment in God

We shared, too, the pain of living out the reality of fulfillment in God outside the "protection" of Yeldall Manor: learning to live with Christian families and secular work environments, learning to grow to maturity in the local church through meeting regularly with people for worship and teaching. Perhaps the biggest shock of learning to live with other Christians, however, was to find that they weren't very open about themselves or very lovingly realistic about others. (In fact, we sometimes got the impression that they would have gained immeasurably from spending a month or more at our center themselves!) What many people did give very freely, however, was love and warmth. Alongside this was an openness to learn from the rich experience that "ex-residents" had to offer.

Compulsive dependency is not easy to break free from—for us. But it is easy for God, so long as we let him do it his way. We have to learn to live like Jesus and that takes time, but God has answers for every situation and he "is faithful; he will not let you be tempted beyond what you can bear. But when you are tempted, he will also provide a way out so that you can stand up under it" (1 Corinthians 10:13).

▼ Power from God

The Bible also reminds us that, in God's love and tenderness toward us, "his divine power has given us everything we need for life and godliness through our knowledge of him who called us by his own glory and goodness. Through these he has given us his very great and precious promises, so that through them you may participate in the divine nature and escape the corruption in the world caused by evil desires" (2 Peter 1:3-4).

So, as you face up to the fact of doing something about your dependency problem, you can be confident that God has already done the groundwork. You can escape the "corruption" of the old life because of what God has done *and* what God has promised. The foundation for your new life not only is laid by God, it has a living foundation—Jesus. But having said this, you need to begin to live in the reality of what he has done and will do. You need to choose to put into practice, to apply the truth in everyday circumstances, so you can actually change. The first practical thing you need to do is to have your mind transformed, to begin to "fill your mind with those things that are good and that deserve praise: things that are true, noble, right, pure, lovely, and honorable" (Philippians 4:8, *Good News Bible*).

▼ Practical steps—transforming our minds

The world has thrown a lot of garbage at us in our lives and many would say that the computer experts' adage "garbage in, garbage out" could probably apply to us. The problem is that we've got a lot of rubbish inside our heads that needs dealing with. Something's got to happen to change all the evil desires, all the garbage, all the distorted lessons we've learned from so many different sources. What we need to do is to feed something into our minds that brings order out of chaos so that we're not constantly pulled the wrong way by distorted messages and pictures from our minds.

Thankfully, the way to get our minds transformed isn't related directly to how much effort we can put into it. Thinking the right things, meditating about good things are important, but without something extra we'll get tired and give up, sooner or later. An important part of the answer is allowing God's supernatural power to transform our minds so that we have "the mind of Christ" (1 Corinthians 2:16). This really can happen when we decide to take seriously the instruction not to "conform any longer to the pattern of this world," but to be "transformed by the renewing of your mind" (Romans 12:2).

The offer of transformation

Charles Colson, one of former President Richard Nixon's right-hand men, became a Christian while serving a prison sentence for his part in the Watergate scandal. He writes:

> The true meaning of the original Greek to transform is that same word from which the English word metamorphosis is derived, and means far more than a natural progressive change, but transformation here is by supernatural means and the only other time that the same word is used in this way in the New Testament is in Matthew 17:2 to describe the transfiguration of Jesus Christ—the Son of God—where "his face shone like the sun and his garments became as white as light."[1]

Colson goes on:

> Man, though still in the flesh, was given a magnificent glimpse of the age to come: the unspeakable joy of literally looking into heaven. This leap from the sin of this world to the holiness of the next is too breathtaking even to contemplate. Yet that is the precise parallel for this passage of Romans: the Christian must make a break with the past so radical that his mind is filled with the thoughts of Christ himself.

Transformation or supernatural renewal comes when we refuse to do things the world's way and learn to read the Bible daily, focusing on those verses that will make us Jesus-oriented men and women. We need to learn to live lives of faith or trust, and that faith "comes from hearing the message, and the message is heard through the word of Christ" (Romans 10:17). Previous patterns and thoughts, distorted by evil desire, are replaced by daily spiritual exercise that results in joy and peace filling our minds.

▼ Practical steps—turning around

As we choose to invite God to renew our minds we will, slowly but surely, begin to feel the old life losing its grip. Gradually, possibly in fits and starts, the life-dominating dependency and the old attitudes and lifestyle will be replaced by fresh, new patterns of thought and behavior.

Meet Helena

For young Helena Wilkinson, an attractive nineteen-year-old woman, a Christian summer camp for young people proved to be a major turning point in her struggle with anorexia. "The end of the summer," she explained later, "brought with it an intense emotional experience, with love and pain intertwined, which had a dramatic effect on me and changed my whole perception of life." Helena became a Christian. She then began to grasp a simple yet profound truth that worked deeply in her life:

God loves you,
which enables

YOU to love YOURSELF
you can then love
OTHERS as YOURSELF
and therefore love
GOD
with all your heart.[2]

Although becoming a Christian is not always an emotional experience for everyone, Helena was in a Christian meeting at the time. "Everyone sang with such deep meaning and the words of the songs moved me deeply," she wrote in her autobiography:

Suddenly I felt a pain shoot through my body; it was as though I was being torn to shreds. I stared straight ahead, tears rolling down my cheeks. I could see Jesus suffering on the cross; what agony he experienced.

Nicky put her arm around me. "Is there anything you want to sing, Helena?" she whispered.

"Jesus, take me as I am; I can come no other way," I replied.

The words moved me deeply. I really wanted Jesus to take me. He died to save me.[3]

The truth that Helena had discovered is something that many Christians don't always fully appreciate immediately. In becoming Christians, we are no longer slaves to the bad or sinful experiences that others have inflicted on us. Neither are we slaves to our own unhealthy and harmful desires and dependencies. The fact is that while the battle might rage on, the ultimate victory has been won by Jesus himself on the cross.

What's going on?

The Christian writer, Derek Prince, sums up the profound significance of the change that takes place within the personality of a person who accepts Jesus as his or her Savior.

> The condition of being dead to sin (Romans 6:11) and living for righteousness (1 Peter 2:24) is something far beyond mere human forgiveness of past sins. In fact, it takes the true believer up into an altogether different realm of spiritual experience. Henceforth he should be dead to sin, but alive to God and to righteousness; he should no longer be a slave of sin; sin should no longer have dominion over him.[4]

In my experience, whenever there is a spiritual step in life, it's wise to follow it up with a practical step. The one goes with the other. Sometimes it involves the very painful act of saying we're sorry to someone we have hurt. Even more painful is the need to forgive someone who has hurt us.

Baptism in water has been another very significant event in the lives of some people who have had life-dominating dependency problems. They have used it not only as a public proclamation of all that God has done to save them, but also to confirm that they are now going to live on God's terms and in God's power. Whatever we may believe about adult baptism, part of its significance is in the fact that it proclaims a clean break with the past. And, whether it is right for us or not, the principle of turning around is very important for release.

As we go under the water, we *choose* to be dead to sin. As we come up out of the water, we not only believe what God has done—that we are no longer a slave to sin—but that we are making an *active* statement that we will now choose righteousness.

▼ Spiritual breakthrough—the Spirit's power

Any practical step, whether it is destroying drugs or burning pornographic magazines, is no real substitute for having our minds renewed. Unless we can say with the apostle Paul that "I no longer live, but Christ lives in me. . . ." (Galatians 2:20), then changes in our behavior are going to be very difficult to keep up in our own strength. The Bible talks repeatedly about the need to be constantly filled with the Spirit, without which our practical steps will be little more than empty rituals—rituals that are carried out in high hopes but result in little or no change in us as people.

For Helena Wilkinson the turning around of her food problem started at her conversion, although she still had a long, long way to go to full recovery. Others that I work with find the public act of baptism a precious and powerful step in their struggle for recovery from drug and alcohol problems. And still others have sensed the Lord beautifully enveloping them with his Spirit and his love so that they are able, over a period of time, to become free from the grip of drugs, gambling, pornography, or petty theft. Please don't minimize the truth of this—*we need to ask for God's Holy Spirit, the Spirit of Jesus, to work deeply in our lives and to search us out. Then we can look forward to change with hope and confidence, not only because we've tried hard, but also because we have responded to God's Word and he has filled us with himself.*

Talking takes guts

If you are sensing your need of the Lord's help with dependency, then talk to someone who understands. This won't always be easy. It takes guts. At first it will be intensely embarrassing to share your innermost thoughts and activities with another person. You will feel very vulnerable. That is why the person needs to be someone you can trust, like a good friend, a counselor, a doctor, or a Christian minister. But the very act of sharing your problems shows to yourself and to God that you are serious about sorting things out once and for all. It will be the beginning of rolling back the years of misery. It will bring healing to broken relationships and a life with other people. It is a brave step of faith, but one that will bring a tremendous sense of relief in itself. It is the beginning of the end.

It may be, however, that you feel the size of your problem is that of a huge supertanker that takes several miles to turn around at sea. You may have tried before and failed, but if you humbly take simple steps of faith, then the Lord can help in wonderful ways. Your life *can* turn around. Then the Holy Spirit will help you to say with real honesty, "I no longer live, but Christ lives in me. The life I live in the body, I live by faith in the Son of God, who loved me and gave himself for me" (Galatians 2:20).

▼ Practical steps—putting off and putting on

A famous prime minister once said, "You may have to fight a battle more than once to win it," and there's more than a grain of truth in this for those breaking free from life-dominating dependency. Whatever the great and glorious promises God has laid down for our new life in Christ, there are some habits that you will find die hard. This is because our minds have got used to desiring specific things to meet our distorted needs, and so we don't let them go too easily. "I don't mind fleeing temptation so long as I can leave a forwarding address" sums up the situation. Sometimes we can laugh at the truth of that statement; at other times we'll want to cry. The important thing, however, is to remember that there is always something we can do to allow the Spirit of Jesus the freedom to move more readily in our lives. We can start each new day or activity, for instance, with the old American slave prayer, "Lord, help me to understand that you ain't going to let nothing come my way that you and me together can't handle."

Getting rid of the old self

Having said all this though, some of us know our way around the "sewers" so well that while we don't like living there, it's more comfortable than doing something about it. So we need to get the right "handle" from the Word of God on new ways of actually doing things. One very powerful life-transforming truth that has been used by many is that we need to engage our minds actively in getting rid of "your old self" and then "put on the new self, created to be like God in true righteousness and holiness" (Ephesians 4:22-24). In other words, there is a standard of living laid down by God that is non-optional. That which is unacceptable to God must be put off or gotten rid of. Some people have found out the hard way that only "putting off" will leave a vacuum that all sorts of garbage could float into. So we must learn to ask God what he wants us to "put on" in place of that which is unacceptable to him.

If we read Ephesians 4 further we will see that Paul gives some practical examples. He suggests, for instance, that we shouldn't only "put off," or stop lying, but "put on," or go out of our way to speak truth. Another example is of someone who used to make his living stealing. He must not only "steal no longer but must work, doing something useful with his own hands, that he may have something to share with those in need" (Ephesians 4:28). As we allow our minds to be transformed, there will be other ways in which we will learn to put off the old, remembering that the new will be created in God's likeness.

Nothing but a slob

Yvonne Sybring wrote in an article called "I Couldn't Start Eating" (*HIS*, May, 1983) about one very real and desperate situation she found herself in.

One summer day came a turning point. I had just made myself a perfectly delicious, nutritious lunch and had brought it into the back yard to eat. Just as I was about to take the first bite, those accusing "voices" began to scream inside my head.

"You don't need that!" they shouted. "You're just a big, fat pig!"

My heartbeat quickened. *Yes, yes, you're right,* I thought. *I'm losing control. I'm nothing but a slob.*

Perspiring, I stood up and looked around wildly, searching for a place to bury my food. I'd carefully prepared the meal, and my body needed it desperately—but all I wanted to do was dig a hole in the garden to hide the food.

I would have done it too, but at that moment a Bible verse popped into my head. It wasn't a verse I recalled memorizing, but there it was: "If the Son sets you free, you will be free indeed" (John 8:36). Immediately another verse came to mind: "For God hath not given us the spirit of fear; but of power, and of love, and of a sound mind" (2 Timothy 1:7, KJV). I knew God was speaking to me through both verses, and I knew what I had to do. Right there I fell to my knees and began to thank him for my food, for my freedom, for the power to eat and enjoy the meal.

For the next nine months I repeated this process, depending on God's Spirit to give me the power to eat. I was gradually learning to depend on him. Slowly my weight increased, and my fear of eating subsided.

It was nine long months, but when it was over God had healed me of anorexia nervosa. Today, three years later, he has also taught me to accept myself. No longer do I rage against him for my "ugliness"—I can see some flaws, but also some good points. And I try to yield all of them to him.

After my experience with anorexia, I'll always know that God exists. After all, he fought for my survival when I was little more than a scarecrow— and he won.

There are so many other practical things that we can do to grow in Christ—not least of all is to join with other Christians. We'll look at fellowship and other practical hints in the next chapter.

▼ Life on God's terms

In the meantime our Father longs for us to be very practical and to follow the example of his Son, Jesus, and choose to serve others. "Be kind and compassionate to one another, forgiving each other, just as in Christ God forgave you" (Ephesians 4:32).

Learning to serve others and especially those who have hurt us in the past, is one of the hardest things of all to do. However, if Jesus could do it, knowing that our sin would crucify him, then so can we. In fact it's the only way we can know all the deepest fulfillment we've ever looked for in our life-dominating dependency. We won't do it by telling ourselves "it's a good idea, but . . ." When we choose to follow Jesus in loving others and putting them first we will experience a reward we never dreamed possible.

Choosing life on God's terms never will be easy, but experiencing the life of God through serving others is a "high" that can never be beaten by anything else on earth.

▼ ▼ ▼

Overcoming doubt and temptation

Everyone, even the most "together" person, has doubts and temptations that threaten to knock him or her off balance. Jesus himself was tempted, especially to doubt God, but he responded simply by reminding the devil what God's Word said.

We, too, can face doubt and temptation head-on by reminding ourselves of what God's Word says. We can meditate on God's Word so that our minds are reminded of truth and not the devil's lies. My favorite verse, which still helps me a lot in difficult situations, is Galatians 2:20 because it reminds me "I have been crucified with Christ and I no longer live, but Christ lives in me. The life I live in the body, I live by faith in the Son of God, who loved me and gave himself for me."

Here are some difficult situations we may face, with verses from the Bible that we can use to get them in perspective.

When we're looking for an excuse to sin
No temptation has seized you except what is common to man. And God is faithful; he will not let you be tempted beyond what you can bear. But when you are tempted, he will also provide a way out so that you can stand up under it. *1 Corinthians 10:13*

When we think we are trapped
So if the Son sets you free, you will be free indeed. *John 8:36*

When we are fearful

For God did not give us a spirit of timidity, but a spirit of power, of love and of self-discipline. *2 Timothy 1:7*

When we doubt God's love

But he was pierced for our transgressions, he was crushed for our iniquities; the punishment that brought us peace was upon him, and by his wounds we are healed. We all, like sheep, have gone astray, each of us has turned to his own way; and the LORD has laid on him the iniquity of us all. *Isaiah 53:5-6*

When we think we're too sinful

Here is a trustworthy saying that deserves full acceptance: Christ Jesus came into the world to save sinners . . . *1 Timothy 1:15*

When we think we're going to fail

But the Lord is faithful, and he will strengthen and protect you from the evil one. *2 Thessalonians 3:3*

When we believe we're too weak

But he said to me, "My grace is sufficient for you, for my power is made perfect in weakness." Therefore I will boast all the more gladly about my weaknesses, so that Christ's power may rest on me. That is why, for Christ's sake, I delight in weaknesses, in insults, in hardships, in persecutions, in difficulties. For when I am weak, then I am strong. *2 Corinthians 12:9-10*

When we believe we've failed

If we confess our sins, he is faithful and just and will forgive us our sins and purify us from all unrighteousness. *1 John 1:9*

When it's difficult to pray

So I say to you: Ask and it will be given to you; seek and you will find; knock and the door will be opened to you. For everyone who asks receives; he who seeks finds; and to him who knocks, the door will be opened. Which of you fathers, if your son asks for a fish, will give him a snake instead? Or if he asks for an egg, will give him a scorpion? If you then, though you are evil, know how to give good gifts to your children, how much more will your Father in heaven give the Holy Spirit to those who ask him! *Luke 11:9-13*

When we're tempted

Consider it pure joy, my brothers, whenever you face trials of many kinds, because you know that the testing of your faith develops perseverance. Perseverance must finish its work so that you may be mature and complete, not lacking anything. *James 1:2-4*

When we're suffering for choosing Jesus

Blessed are those who are persecuted because of righteousness, for theirs is the kingdom of heaven. Blessed are you when people insult you, persecute you and falsely say all kinds of evil against you because of me. Rejoice and be glad, because great is your reward in heaven, for in the same way they persecuted the prophets who were before you. *Matthew 5:10-12*

6

*B*reaking free

Almost every person I have met who had a life-dominating dependency problem has been a highly intelligent and acutely sensitive individual. Each had tried, over and over, to break free but had always failed—in the end. They failed, in nine cases out of ten, because the only choice they made was to give up the drink, the drugs, the pornography, or whatever. They hadn't realized, and no one had told them, that just stopping a certain behavior changes nothing. They were only ex-addicts who no longer took drugs, only ex-alcoholics who never drank, only ex-gamblers who resisted gambling. As soon as a major problem came, they found themselves taking the only option they knew to make themselves feel better. Even becoming a Christian simply to stop using drugs or gambling wasn't enough. Christianity was simply a crutch that they hoped would stop them from falling over.

▼ Choices and changes

Real transformation began when they wanted to be
something different. It wasn't a question of changing
their image so that other people thought they were
different. It was making the decision to change from
the inside, and realizing that they couldn't do it
without Christ's help.

Once they had reached this conclusion, they were
not only going further and further away from their
addiction or dependency, but were becoming more
like Christ, more like the person God created them to
be.

Another critical choice that makes the difference
between talking about change and actually changing,
is to *do* something. Everyone has many different
things that they are going to do sometime in the
future. Yet few people actually achieve everything they
dream about doing.

For the person with a compulsive dependency problem, it is absolutely vital that he or she doesn't just
dream but does something *practical.* It may even be
as important as to start doing something or die.
Sounds dramatic, doesn't it? Yet for people who are
dependent on drugs or alcohol and who have anorexia
or bulimia, the facts are stark and clear.

▼ Practical steps to making the break

The practical steps that follow are given as a very
general guideline, but they may help you toward
breaking completely free.

1. Don't try to do it on your own

Pride has often been at the very root of our compulsive dependency, especially when it comes to admitting we've got a problem. Choosing to be different gives us the freedom to start looking for people who can help us break free.

A good place to start asking for help, apart from the list at the back of this book, is with those nearest to us, who have probably been praying and wanting to help us for a long time. After parents and friends, it may be helpful to see a doctor who can then monitor what's happening to us.

People who have been through the same life-dominating dependency problems can also give a great deal of sound advice and support, as well as alerting us to the danger signs that may appear in our lives if we get complacent or impatient.

One important place to find help and support is a local church, where the people involved are also on the same journey. In other words, they have accepted themselves for who and what they are, but they want to be different, they want to be like Jesus. Local churches will vary quite a lot in many different ways, so don't be afraid to try them all. The clues to those that are worth investigating further are those where:

- You are welcomed for who you are and made to feel comfortable and at home.

- The teaching is based on the Bible.

- The person leading the service or preaching is sincere and believes in what he or she is saying.

- The people inside look happier than those outside.

- You are invited to activities outside the church by those inside, sooner or later.

- Eventually you feel able to share something of yourself, if not your real needs and problems.

Keeping these general guidelines in mind, don't try to find the perfect church, because there isn't one. The only thing that's perfect is Jesus, and he's still working with his people.

Whoever is trying to help you, be realistic and be vulnerable because until you are, no one can give you the support and help you really need. Don't forget that those who want to help you have needs, too, and an occasional thank-you from you will reinforce and build up the relationship between you both. If you fail someone, then remember that he or she will probably be as eager, or more eager, to mend the relationship as you are. Saying you're sorry always brings healing.

2. Withdrawing in the right environment
If you have a compulsive dependency problem, then you will probably have a good idea of what withdrawing from the problem is all about. You have tried plenty of times before, but have found the discomfort too great to handle most times and found the only way of coping was to go back to the same habitual behavior. Somehow, though, if you are going to break completely free, you are going to have to make the choice to stop—and therefore choose to go through the discomfort.

Prayer can also make a very significant difference in the withdrawal process. I have personally seen people suffer far fewer withdrawal symptoms, or even none at all, when they have prayed with me or others.

Physical withdrawal, particularly where food has been abused, needs to be done with the awareness of a medical expert. Here again, prayer can be significant alongside the slow adjusting of mealtimes and diets.

Action to deal with pornography or gambling, as well as drugs and drink, must involve the removal and destruction (to ensure innocent parties don't become involved) of any substance or material that may be a temptation. There should be no compromise of any description if you really want complete freedom.

It will help to involve other people in your withdrawal in order to be completely successful. Be completely realistic with them about what to expect and especially those ways in which you know you could manipulate them to get your own way if you get desperate. If necessary, hand over your wallet, credit cards, and even the control of your bank account if that is the only way you can prevent yourself from slipping back into bondage to compulsive dependency. When it comes to withdrawal, the more open and realistic you are with yourself and other people, the more likely you are to break free and *stay* free.

3. The importance of radical amputation

Radical amputation simply means doing everything necessary to cut yourself off from those people, circumstances, and places that could draw you back into compulsive attitudes, habits, or behavior. You know better than anyone how deceitful you can be when under pressure, and again, it is your level of openness that will dictate how quickly and effectively you break free.

If it means ensuring that someone supervises all your movements for a time, this is worthwhile. In the early stages of recovery, they can help you to stay away from wrong areas or even specific shops if need be. They also can assist you in avoiding certain people who, by their lifestyle, will lead you to fall into temptation.

For some this radical amputation may even go as far as moving to a new house or changing jobs. But if that's what it's going to take for you to find complete freedom, joy, and fulfillment in your life, then it will all be worthwhile.

4. Making the break

Here are some practical ideas to work through to ensure you really do break free:

a. *Positively adjust your timetable.* Take an honest look at the normal activities of the day and week ahead. Review them one by one and take steps to do the right thing so you won't be tempted to do the wrong thing. For instance, you may know that walking along a certain road each day creates the wrong feelings in you. Make the choice to go a different way, even if it involves a longer walk. Once you have each day carefully mapped out, then look at the week ahead.

Take a careful look at obvious times of danger. For some these are mealtimes, while for others it will be a Friday or Saturday night when they normally go out for a "good time." Take steps to organize something completely different, such as spending the evening with friends.

b. *Tone up your mind and your body.* Make positive changes in what you hear, what you see, and what you eat. Remember that "garbage in" means you will be more likely to want to slip into old, dangerous patterns of behavior. Recognizing negative talk from others for what it is and quietly walking away can only be helpful to you, and to them. Choosing a different newspaper to avoid certain pictures, or turning the television off before an offensive program means that you won't have to go through the pressure of battling with temptation. Choosing to eat the right foods at the right times may be difficult, but it really is good to know that you have made the right decision.

Remember, too, that apart from the long-term benefits, regular exercise can be extremely helpful, particularly at stress times, by taking your mind off thoughts and events that will possibly bring you down again.

c. *Set realistic targets.* Plan to get yourself successfully through the next hour instead of telling yourself how different things will be in a week or a month's time. When you're through that first hour, then thank God for all the blessings that have come from being free for that hour. Then go through the next hour, then the next, until you can rejoice in a whole day of being free.

Don't live your life according to other people's expectations—real or imagined. Weigh carefully what other people say. Try out those suggestions you know are realistic. Put other ideas that don't seem right at a particular time to one side to try later.

d. *When you can't help remembering the pleasure, remind yourself of the misery.* Remind yourself regularly of the pain, misery, and despair of your compulsive dependency and just how dreadful it really was. Tell yourself the truth—that it really was all a facade. Be realistic—it never met any deep needs. Remind yourself, for instance, in a letter to yourself, how life really was when you were hooked.

Remember, too, all the hurt and distress that others have been through because you kept choosing wrongly. Thank God that those same people want to help you now. Choose to go through the discomfort of saying no to yourself so that other people can have less pressure and more hope.

▼ Spiritual steps to breaking free

Spiritual steps are as critically important to breaking free from compulsive dependency as practical steps. What goes on in our minds is far more likely to dictate what we do with our bodies than the other way around.

God not only gave us the bodies that we have (Psalm 139:13), but our bodies are also temples of the Holy Spirit of God (1 Corinthians 6:19).

John Throop, in an article called "I Lost It," wrote:

> The Hebrews didn't try to separate body, soul and spirit. All are of the same creation, and all have the same value before God. What we do with our bodies affects our spiritual lives. The reverse is true as well. That's why we need to take a spiritual inventory of our physical desires. If we hope for the peace of Christ in our lives, for wholeness and health, we must commit both our spiritual and our physical lives to the Lord.[1]

He goes on to reinforce this issue further:

He [God] wants us to proclaim with our bodies what we proclaim with our spiritual lives. In the end there is no difference between the two. If we cannot bring our bodies under the firm and loving control of Christ, then we will forever be spiritually undernourished. God wants us to use our bodies rightly. "You are not your own," Paul says, "you were bought with a price. So glorify God in your body" (1 Corinthians 6:19-20).

Glorifying God is what we were created for, and we can move into every measure of peace, joy, and fulfillment as we learn to take the following spiritual steps day by day.

1. Read the Bible regularly

If there's something we always need more of, it is faith in the knowledge of God to enable us to live life dependency-free and in all its fullness. "Faith comes from hearing the message" (Romans 10:17), and the message, read daily in the Bible, results in more faith and our ongoing growth and development into the likeness of Christ.

Learn one or two verses from the Bible that you can repeat when the pressure gets really hot. One of the verses that helped me find genuine freedom and that I used to repeat over and over when I was under pressure was "I no longer live, but Christ lives in me. The life I live in the body, I live by faith in the Son of God, who loved me and gave himself for me" (Galatians 2:20). The more I repeated those words in my mind, the more easily I was able to focus on the situation I was in. As well as that, I was able to delight in the fact that God's Spirit chose to live in me and was going to enable me to respond in the right way, his way.

As you come across verses in the Bible that really come alive to you and your circumstances, then underline them so that you can find them later when you want to be reminded about what they say.

2. Deal with resentment from the past

Saying we're sorry to God for the things we've done wrong doesn't always mean we forgive those who have hurt us. Ask God to reveal those things that he wants you to deal with, then ask him to replace any debt you believe people owe you with love for them.

Ask God to make you aware of those things that you have done wrong to other people and that are still causing them distress. Once we are clear exactly what it is we've done wrong, then we need to ask God how he wants us to put it right so we can live in the joy of a clear conscience. Remember that apologizing, by letter if we can't do it verbally, can replace the hurt and bitterness with love and forgiveness. The important thing is to apologize without trying to justify anything.

Keep a short account with God for other people in the future. Deal with resentment as soon as it begins by remembering that God is big enough to use those things that other people do unwittingly, as well as deliberately, for our good. Ask God for ways in which you can respond in a Christlike manner so he can change them, in his way.

3. When you're tempted, look for God's way

God's Word clearly tells us that, as long as we really want to do things his way, we're not going to be tested beyond our power to remain firm. God loves you far too much to allow you to get into a situation you can't handle. At such times, though, "he will also provide a way out so that you can stand up under it" (1 Corinthians 10:13).

4. Seek God's righteousness
Seek to do everything in a way that is right—as far as God is concerned. If you do this faithfully in every circumstance, then not only will you become totally free, but God will provide everything else you need (Matthew 6:33).

5. Enjoy God's "treats"
I have not the slightest doubt that, like many an earthly father, God will give you "treats." The blessing comes not only in accepting them for what they are, but in looking forward to other ways in which God is going to "treat" you out of his love in the days ahead.

6. If you fail, remember God forgives
As soon as you recognize that you have failed, ask for God's forgiveness. Don't try to fool him, though. God knows that we've gotten used to apologizing just to get people off our backs. The repentance that God wants, because he wants us to be free, is when we are so sorry that we don't want to do the same thing again. When we truly do repent, God not only forgives us but forgets all about the wrong as well (Isaiah 43:25).

If you keep failing, however, talk it through with another Christian, and ask him or her to pray with you as well as help you work out practical ways of overcoming the particular problem. Sharing helps lift the added pain of suffering and struggling alone, and God will use it to bless the other person as well.

7. Find the freedom from God to "be thankful in all circumstances"

You can't be any freer, on this earth, than to get through to the place where you truly can look at any situation, no matter how difficult, and find something in it to thank God for. It will take time to be able to do that in some cases, but God's Word says that is what God wants for our lives—so that makes it possible.

It's that place where we can truly say, in faith, I know "that in all things God works for the good of those who love him" (Romans 8:28). Nothing harmful can ever really make much difference to you when you discover the secret of this verse.

It means, too, according to Philippians 4:7, that we will not only know "the peace of God, which transcends all understanding" but that same peace "will guard your hearts and your minds in Christ Jesus."

Go after freedom like this—it's worth all the wealth in the world. Jesus died for us so that we can know freedom, and he doesn't need to do it again so that we can know resurrection life like his.

7

*H*elping someone break free

Empathy, compassion, tenderness, and a quiet strength are absolutely essential in helping others break free from a life-dominating compulsion or infatuation. Yet strangely, the most effective people in this work are often the last to recognize these Christlike qualities in themselves. During my ten years of experience in this area I have come to realize that without humility before God, a desire for personal righteousness, and a knowledge of his love and power, little can be achieved that is long-lasting.

The guidelines in this chapter are designed for the non-expert who wants to be a friend to someone who is struggling. If a relationship becomes difficult or a problem begins to get out of hand, then ease out of the situation quickly. This is better than disappointing someone later on when the stakes are higher. It is not a sign of failure or lack of faith in God to admit that a friend's compulsion or infatuation is too big for

an amateur to cope with. Seek professional help
sooner rather than later. Don't try to be a hero; you
might need to be needed—a dependency in itself.

What follows is not foolproof, but the ideas can
save many hours of trial and error. Each will need
adapting to suit different people and varying situations.

Remember, above all, that you're not dealing with a
problem, whether it's drugs, alcohol, pornography, or
anything else, but with a *person*. You won't change
the problems; they will always be there. But God has
answers for people's lives no matter how complex,
how distorted they may be. More than this, God loves
the person you are helping more than you and I can
ever love him or her. He desires to be intimately
involved in his or her life, and he pours all the
resources of heaven into bringing that person through
to freedom.

With this in mind, we can look with confidence to
some basic guidelines that can help bring about the
freedom we're all looking for.

1. Build a relationship

One of the most important ways we can help others is
by acknowledging them as fellow human beings—just
as they are. Demonstrating acceptance of them by
saying hello, or greeting them by name every time we
see them, can go a long way in laying down a foundation of trust and respect for one another.

Don't worry if the process of getting to know someone takes time. Remember that, as long as we're
ready and willing to listen, God not only will tell us
when to do something, but he will also engineer the
circumstances to hasten the process.

2. Pray and get others praying

Prayer will always be the "secret weapon," the means of bridging the gap between circumstances as they are now and the way God wants them to be. It is especially relevant when the going is toughest. Time and again it will increase understanding, it will break barriers down and ensure that the progress begins again.

Because prayer changes things, it's important that other people are not only praying for the person you are helping but for you as well. You need wisdom, insight, sensitivity, love, hope, and joy—get people to pray that those things will be a reality in your life.

3. Reinforce hope

Encouragement will be vital at every stage of breaking free—and after. Constantly look and pray for ways of reinforcing hope. Especially praise the person you're helping for every positive step he or she makes, no matter how tiny.

Remember particularly to reinforce hope by telling the person you're helping that if God could change you, then he or she has got all the hope in the world!

4. Be realistic

Be realistic, too, about the real measure of how much needs changing—especially about the attitudes he or she holds, which might be totally unfamiliar or might take time to turn around. Here are some commonly held views:

- The world really does owe me a living.

- Getting something for nothing is success.

- Anything is fair in love and war.

- It's more blessed to get than to give.

- The end justifies any means.

- Whatever is yours is mine—especially if it's insured.

- I may be a mess, but it's everyone else's fault.

- Why should I change when everyone else is such a hypocrite?

Realism about your own life will help the person be realistic about his or her life. False realism, however, that fails to face up to real issues, will only result in failure. Anything we do selfishly to make ourselves feel better must always be suspect. We can afford to face up to just how difficult a situation is without pretending or feeling insecure, by remembering that God is in control and wants the person we're helping to be totally free.

5. Don't get irritated (too much!)
Be wise to his or her manipulation of you, your emotions, and circumstances, while learning to be consistent in a gentle but firm response. If this person mistreats you or other people, draw the line. Point out that such behavior is unacceptable. It not only hurts others, but demeans the person you're helping as well.

When all else fails, and the anger and frustration are building up to the point where you're worried you'll explode, ask God to put it in the only place capable of being unaffected by it—his Father heart.

6. Be vulnerable

If you're not prepared to be vulnerable, to be real, how can you expect the person you are helping to be? Being real about your own inadequacy and failure will do more to convince him or her of your commitment and love than all the other words and actions put together.

Apologize if you're wrong. Very few people have ever done that, and it will bring results beyond anything you can believe.

7. Be prepared to say no

Don't be a doormat, especially when it's going to result in the person being tempted. For example, don't give money if he or she will probably spend it on drugs, drink, gambling, or whatever, Buy a bag of groceries or a travel ticket to wherever he or she is going.

Say no when he or she is taking advantage of other people's good natures.

8. Make appointments

You can't help someone very much if he or she doesn't want to change. Part of testing motivation, whether someone wants to carry on breaking free or not, is by you both making and keeping appointments. (If the person is drunk, write it down and let him or her keep it. Don't go looking if he or she doesn't turn up.) Remember, everyone has a choice, and if he or she doesn't want any more help, you can't force it.

When you next see the person, make it clear you missed seeing him or her and *ask* whether he or she wants to make another arrangement for you to talk, go to the doctor, or whatever.

9. Talk about Jesus
Tell the person about Jesus and his love for him or her—just as he or she is. Talk, too, about how God created him or her as a unique personality and has a perfect place for his or her life, free from dependency and finding fulfillment in serving others.

10. Trust in God's Spirit to bring about change
Our words about Jesus, no matter how passionate, won't bring change. Only God's Holy Spirit brings conviction "in regard to sin and righteousness and judgment" (John 16:8).

Trust God's Spirit, too, in his power to bring peace and release through prayer. God has told us that we can minister the supernatural reality of Jesus (Acts 4:30), which brings with it an awareness of God that can never be dismissed again. Don't however, try to use spiritual "exercise" to compensate for lack of commitment or long-term support on your part. God's power needs to be used in the context of holiness in our lives and selfless love for the one we are helping. But when God says to move, then expect great things to happen. Enjoy finding out that God's power is not limited by how much you believe.

11. Remember there is always an option
The person you are helping has gained relief and release from the pressures of living by adopting a compulsive habitual behavior. For this reason, he or

she will not only be tempted to revert to that behavior, but it will always be an option when life gets tough. That is why your commitment has to be long-term and consistent, so that the person knows there is someone to stand with him or her in the pain of saying no—to themselves.

12. Don't try to counsel when someone is "high"
Trying to communicate with someone who is under the influence of drugs, alcohol, or lack of food is always counter-productive and should be avoided. If he or she doesn't want help enough to turn up for a meeting "straight," then arrange another meeting—and pray.

13. Discuss the possibility of change
Discussion about the next *realistic* step that someone needs to take, whether it's change of heart, mind, or lifestyle, is important. Remember, however, to keep it to discussion only, until you both believe that the person is ready, and able, to do what you have agreed successfully. To move too fast may reinforce failure, and failure has probably been a major feature of that person's life almost since the cradle.

14. Look at realistic alternatives
What are the alternatives you can offer in relation to the person's need and experience of instant gratification? How are the terms we use—joy and fulfillment, order and structure, peace of mind, etc. to be translated into realistic options? If you don't know the answer to these questions, why should the person you're helping pursue them? Furthermore, if your life doesn't reflect the reality of these things, then why

should he or she change anyway? If the lives of the people you introduce them to don't reflect that reality, why should they listen to what you say?

15. Involve other people
At the beginning of these guidelines we talked about other people praying for the person in need. Whether these other people have been involved earlier or not, they certainly need to be from now on, mainly because they will confirm or deny the love and acceptance you have been showing to the person you've been helping.

(One word of caution when involving other people, though. Introduce someone to a couple of people over a cup of coffee before taking them into a larger group. Only take someone to church, for instance, when there will be at least six people there that he or she knows well enough to chat with.)

16. Counsel for direct change
Keep checking what cure he or she really wants. People with compulsive dependencies are good at having great plans, but, like the rest of us, not so good at achieving them. It may also be that all he or she really wants to do is:

- Find a little comfort.

- Recoup enough resources to carry on with his or her compulsive behavior.

- Try to avoid the consequences of a custodial sentence or financial ruin.

Help to clarify the person's thinking by leading him or her to talk about realities, not fantasies, and discuss the consequences of what he or she is proposing to do.

17. Discuss "radical amputation"
The need to get completely away from his or her immediate home environment and wrong friends will be an important part in making the break. Failure to provide realistic alternatives in terms of somewhere else to live, in particular, is one of the biggest reasons why so many people fail to break free of life-dominating dependency.

One of the only organizations capable of providing the resources of an alternative family, home, and friends is the local church. It would be foolish to disguise the difficulties involved in providing such an extensive level of support and supervision, but thankfully, groups of Christians are readily providing them.

18. Don't disguise the difficulties
Don't attempt to entice anyone to change by trying to make everything appear too easy—it will always backfire on you both. It's also dishonest and will take a lot of renewed effort. If, having been brutally realistic about a course of action, he or she wants to carry on, then the plan will be far more likely to be successful.

Offering some radical change can bring justifiable fear. Accepting the fear for what it is—not simply someone being negative—will bring opportunities to speak God's truth and solutions into the situation. Don't belittle, but continue to show love, support, and (especially) your conviction in what God wants to do on his or her behalf.

19. Keep on loving and reinforcing hope

God never treats failure by withdrawing his love, and
we have no right to be different from him. Perhaps
one of the most important lessons you'll have to learn
is the same one that many others have learned the
hard way—that you, personally, don't have enough
love to fill the vacuum in others. Thankfully, when
you admit this to God, he pours in the love of Jesus,
and, in him, there's a never-ending supply.

Finally, when it comes to practical guidelines in
helping others, keep reminding yourself of God's plan
for the person you're helping, which is clearly stated
in God's Word:

> that the body of Christ may be built up until we all
> reach unity in the faith and in the knowledge of the
> Son of God and become mature, attaining to the
> whole measure of the fullness of Christ. *Ephesians
> 4:12-13*

Resources

Before looking for help, remember that it may already be close at hand in the form of:

- Your local, understanding church—where a minister will help you, or know of someone who can.
- Your local doctor—who will have the right information for your particular situation.

In the United States:

Local chapters of national support groups such as Alcoholics Anonymous and Over-Eaters Anonymous can be found in your local telephone directory in the community service section under general headings (alcoholism, drug abuse, eating disorders).

Alcohol/drug abuse

Alcoholics for Christ
1316 North Campbell Road
Royal Oak, MI 48067
800-441-7877
Nondenominational, nonprofit, evangelical fellowship for substance abusers and their families.

Ephesians 5:18
Life Ministries
1620 Elton Road, Suite 204
Silver Spring, MD 2090
301-439-7191
Provides a twelve-step program, testing and clinical group
work for substance abusers and their families.

National Federation of Parents for Drug-Free Youth
800-554-KIDS

National Referral Hotline
800-COCAINE

Overcomers Outreach, Inc.
2290 W. Whittier Blvd.,
Suite A-D
La Habra, CA 90631
213-697-3994
Nonprofit ministry of support groups to chemically dependent people, their family members, and friends.

Parents Resource for Drug Education
(PRIDE)
800-241-9746

Treatment programs

National Teen Challenge
1525 N. Campbell Avenue
Springfield, MO 65803
417-862-6969
Offers drug and alcohol treatment programs.

New Life for Girls
RD 3, Box D700
Dover, PA 17315
717-266-5414

New Life Ministries
Suite 140
7900 Plaza Blvd. #188
Mentor, OH 44060-5517
216-946-7037 or 216-257-7103
Nonprofit organization offering retreats, workshops, support groups, and seminars on drug and alcohol abuse, co-dependency, and related issues.

New Life Treatment Centers
570 Glenneyre, Suite 107
Laguna Beach, CA 92651
1-800-227-LIFE
1-800-332-TEEN (Hotlines)
Several centers with tracks for drug and alcohol addictions, eating addictions, sexual addictions, and general psychological disorders that focus on the Twelve Steps. Programs for adults and adolescents are available.

Walter Hoving Home for Women
P.O. Box 194
Garrison, NY 10524
914-424-3674
A one-year school promoting Christian growth for substance-abusing women 18–55.

Pornography and the media

Morality in Media
475 Riverside Drive, Suite 239
New York, NY 10115
212-870-3222
National organization to stop pornography through education and enforcement of laws. Provides legal information to prosecutors and other interested attorneys.

National Coalition against Pornography
800 Compton Road
Suite 9224
Cincinnati, OH 45231
513-521-6227
Alliance of citizens, religious groups and private organizations to eliminate hard-core pornography through education and legal action. Offers a variety of educational materials.

National Coalition on Television Violence
P.O. Box 2157
Champaign, IL 61825-2157
217-384-1920
Monitors TV and movies.

Parents' Music Resource Center
1500 Arlington Boulevard
Suite 300
Arlington, VA 22209
703-527-9466
Nonprofit resource center to educate parents and consumers about violent, pornographic, and pro-drug messages in popular music.

General services

International Union of Gospel Missions
P.O. Box 10780
Kansas City, MO 64118
800-624-5156
Worldwide association of rescue ministries, providing
materials, training, and assistance to urban missions.

*National Directory of Alcoholism & Addiction Treatment
Programs* (including agencies, services, and community
resources)
Published by *Alcoholism and Addiction Magazine*
4959 Commerce Parkway
Cleveland, OH 44128
216-464-1210

Salvation Army
National Headquarters
799 Bloomfield Avenue
Verona, NJ 07044
201-239-0606
International Christian charitable movement providing
personal spiritual counseling and material assistance to
all in need.

Toughlove
P.O. Box 1069
Doylestown, PA 18901
215-348-7090

In the United Kingdom:

Alcohol/drug abuse

Alcoholics Anonymous
(Provides addresses of local AA meetings)
11 Redcliffe Gardens
London SW10
071 352 9779

Narcotics Anonymous
P.O. Box 246
London SW10
071 351 6794

Re-Solv (solvent abuse)
St. Mary's Chambers
Station Road
Stone, Staffs ST15 8JP
0785 46097

The Band of Hope (Christian Education)
25(F) Copperfield Street
London SE1 OEN
071 928 0848

ECOD (Evangelical Coalition on Drugs)
Evangelical Alliance
186 Kennington Park Road
London SW11 4BT
071 582 0228

Treatment programs

Yeldall Christian Centres (male)
Yeldall Manor, Blakes Lane
Hare Hatch, Reading RG10 9XR
0734 402287/404411

Meta House (female, mothers & children)
133 Princess Road
Westbourne, Bournemouth
0202 764581

Coke Hole Trust (male & female)
70 Junction Road
Andover SP10 3QX
0264 61745

Teen Challenge Centre (male)
Penygroes Road
Gorlas, Llanelli
Dyfed SA14 7LA
0269 842718

Adullam Homes (male & female)
The Mount
Lawley Bank
Telford TG4 2JJ
0952 502787

Life for the World (female)
Hebron House
12 Stanley Avenue
Thorpe Hamlet
Norwich NR7 0BE
0603 39905

Kenward House (male—alcohol)
Kenward Road
Yalding, Kent
0622 812 603

Willowdene Farm (male)
Chorley, Nr. Bridgnorth
Shropshire WV16 6PP
074632 658

Eating disorders

Anorexia and Bulimia Care (Christian)
15 Fernhust Gate
Aughton, Lancs L39 5ED
Northern Office: 0695 422479/35318
Southern Office: 0449 740145.

Eating Disorders Association
Sackville Place
Magdalen Street
Norwhich, Norfolk NR3 1JE
0603 621414/0494 21431

Gambling

Gamblers Anonymous
17/23 Blantyre Street
Cheyne Walk
London SW10
Tel: 071 352 3060

General counseling

Association of Biblical Counsellors
ABC, Townsend Chambers, Amherst Hill
Sevenoaks, Kent TN15 6XZ

Ellel Grange
Ellel
Lancaster LA2 OHN
0524 751651

General services

Christian Training Resource:
CWR (Crusade for World Revival)
Waverley Abbey House
Farnham, Surrey GU9 8EP

Christian Support for Professionals
Caring Professions Concern
175 Wokingham Road
Earley, Reading RG6 1LU
0734 660515

Notes

Chapter 1

1. Liz Round, "To Eat or Not to Eat," *21st Century Christian* (August, 1989).
2. Bill Hybels, *Christians in a Sex-Crazed Culture* (Victor Books, 1989).
3. James and Joyce Ditzler, *Living in the Day: Meditations to Help You Through the Year* (Hodder & Stoughton, 1989).

Chapter 2

1. Daisy Waugh, "Starving for Attention," *Woman Magazine.*
2. James and Joyce Ditzler, *Living in the Day.*
3. Liz Round, "To Eat or Not to Eat."
4. From a personal story written by Steve and used at outreach meetings.
5. From a personal story by Roger, told to author.
6. Bill Hybels, *Christians in a Sex-Crazed Culture.*
7. Steve's story, see note 4.

Chapter 3

1. Bill and Joanie Voder, *Got Any Bread?* (Operation Concern, 1976).

2. Virginia Larsen, "Games Eaters Play," *HIS* (May, 1983).
3. Virginia Larsen, "Games Eaters Play."
4. John Powell, *Why Am I Afraid to Love?* (Tabor Publishing, 1967).
5. Lawrence Crabb, *Effective Biblical Counseling* (Marshall Pickering, 1977).
6. Floyd McClung, *The Father Heart of God* (Harvest House, 1985).
7. Lawrence Crabb, *Basic Principles of Christian Counseling* (Marshall Pickering, 1975).
8. Charles Solomon, *Handbook to Happiness* (Tyndale House, 1979).

Chapter 4

1. From a personal testimony supplied by Anorexia and Bulimia Care (see Resources).
2. Lawrence Crabb, *Effective Biblical Counseling*.

Chapter 5

1. Charles Colson, *Life Sentence* (Fleming H. Revell, 1981).
2. Helena Wilkinson, *Puppet on a String* (Hodder & Stoughton, 1984).
3. Helena Wilkinson, *Puppet on a String*.
4. Derek Prince, The Foundation Series, Vol. 2 (Sovereign World, Ltd., 1986).

Chapter 6

1. John Throop, "I Lost It," *HIS* (February, 1989).